LIGHT SPORT AIRCRAFT

INSPECTION
PROCEDURES

KEVIN KOCHERSBERGER

AVOTEK®
INFORMATION RESOURCES

by Kevin Kochersberger

International Standard Book Number 1-933189-06-01
Order # T-LSINPR-0101

For Sale by: Avotek
A Select Aerospace Industries company

Mail to:
P.O. Box 219
Weyers Cave, Virginia 24486
USA

Ship to:
200 Packaging Drive
Weyers Cave, Virginia 24486
USA

Toll Free: 1-800-828-6835
Telephone: 1-540-234-9090
Fax: 1-540-234-9399

Printed in the USA

www.avotekbooks.com

Preface

This book has been written to explain the details of the annual condition inspection for light sport aircraft, with the new owner in mind. I wrote this book for the pilot—someone who is familiar with the preflight inspection, but has not spent a great deal of time under the engine cowl. Light sport aircraft certification brings the aircraft owner the option of performing his/her own annual condition inspections to reduce the cost of flying. These experimentally-certificated light sport aircraft (ELSA) give the owner latitude in maintenance and inspections, with the only training requirement being a 16-hour repairman's course in inspection. Not only is there an economic justification for taking this path, but the owner gains knowledge about how the aircraft operates, making the sport safer.

I have written this book to complement the 16-hour inspection course that allows owners of ELSA to perform their own annual condition inspections. It was originally designed around the FAA's requirements for the inspection course, and as a result, contains sections on regulations as well as inspections. Readers will learn what is required to certificate a light sport aircraft and ensure it is in an airworthy condition. Owners of production light sport aircraft will benefit as well; even if they are not certified to perform maintenance and inspections. These owners will learn how to assess the health of their bird before a problem becomes serious. This book is an invaluable complement to the aircraft's maintenance manual, highlighting safety-of-flight issues and the reasons behind maintenance and inspection procedures.

My experience flying a reproduction Wright 1903 Flyer for the Centennial of Flight Celebration on December 17, 2003 taught me that man and machine must communicate effectively to achieve successful flight. In the case of Wright aircraft, the pilot must continually sense attitude to control the inherent instability of the airframe. In the case of LSA, engines and airframes are not silent; they will usually tell the pilot if something is wrong before a serious problem develops. This book aims to improve your communication skills with aircraft.

This manual is intended to be used primarily for general training and familiarization in an approved light sport aircraft class. The material in this manual is not to be used as a substitute for any data supplied by the manufacturer or approved by the FAA.

Always use the manufacturer's manuals for any inspections or repairs to any ELSA, S-LSA or LSA.

Dedicated to A. Scott Crossfield—pilot, engineer and innovator of advanced aircraft.

Email us at corrections@avotekbooks.com with comments or suggestions. ➤

Avotek® Aircraft Maintenance Series:

Introduction to Aircraft Maintenance
Aircraft Structural Maintenance
Aircraft System Maintenance
Aircraft Powerplant Maintenance

Other Books by Avotek®:

Aircraft Structural Technician
Avotek® Aeronautical Dictionary
Aviation Maintenance Technician Handbook
Aircraft Wiring & Electrical Installation

Acknowledgements

Rick Anderson — *Yankee Composites*

John Baker — *Hangar 9 Aeroworks*

Mark Bayer — *Skychutes, Inc.*

Bob Dart — *Dart Airport*

Gregg Ellsworth — *Ballistic Recovery Systems*

Excalibur Aircraft

Flight Design USA

Flight Star USA

Edsel Ford — *FAA*
(Light Sport Aircraft Regulating Division)

Ken Hyde — *Virginia Aviation & Machine*

John Lasko — *Quicksilver Aircraft*

Otto Lilienthal Museum, Anklam, Germany

Mike Loehle — *Loehle Aircraft Corporation*

Edwin Miller II — *Kappa Aircraft*

Erik Pederson — *Phantom Aeronautics, LLC*

Tom Peghiny — *Flightstar, Inc.*

Ram Pattisapu — *Indus Aviation, Inc.*

Andy Silvester — *Suncoast Sportplanes, Inc.*

Seppo Simula — *lightaircrafts.com*

Van Stumpner — *FAA*
(Light Sport Aircraft Regulating Division)

Solo Aviation

Izek Therrien — *Kolb Sport*

R.I.T. Department of Mechanical Engineering

Rob Rollison — *Rollison Light Sport Aircraft*

Nick Viscio — *Blue Heron Powered Parachutes*

Paul Yarnall — *Technical Resolutions*

Contents

Chapter 1

INTRODUCTION *to light sport aircraft*

Light sport aircraft (LSA) encompass many designs of airplanes, gliders and lighter-than-air aircraft, which are simpler in design and operation than general aviation aircraft. Heavy ultralight designs, which up until now were not classified, are designated as LSA. Many of the emerging aircraft designs that are tailored to LSA promise to account for significant growth in aviation in the next several years. The final rules for certification of aircraft, pilots and repairmen were issued by the Federal Aviation Administration in September, 2004 as part of Title 14 of the Code of Federal Regulations.

Section 1

Types of Light Sport Aircraft

There are several components to the LSA classification. The general characteristics for the LSA designation that are outlined in FAR Part 1-1 are:

- Maximum gross takeoff weight not to exceed 1,320 lb (600 kg).

- For aircraft intended for water operations the weight cannot exceed 1,430 lb (650 kg)

- For lighter than air LSA the maximum gross weight is 660 lbs (300 kg).

- Maximum airspeed in level flight will not exceed 120 kts at sea level, standard atmospheric conditions.

- Maximum stalling speed or minimum steady flight speed without the use of lift-enhancing devices of not more than 45 knots at maximum certificated take-off weight and most critical center of gravity (CG)

Learning Objectives:

- *Types of Light Sport Aircraft*

- *Light Sport Aircraft and the Regulations Governing the Sport Pilot*

- *Special Light Sport Aircraft*

- *Experimental Light Sport Aircraft*

- *Transitioning Ultralights*

- *Pilot Certification*

Left. **The CTsw is one example of a fixed wing light sport aircraft.**

Figure 1-1-1. The T-Bird is an example of an allowed ELSA design.

Figure 1-1-2. The CT2 is a high-end, composite structure LSA.

Figure 1-1-3. Repositionable landing gear on an amphibious LSA.

- Two-passenger maximum

- Single, reciprocating engine only (if powered)

- A fixed- or ground- adjustable propeller (if powered)

- A non-pressurized cabin, if equipped with a cabin

- Fixed landing gear, except for an aircraft intended for operation on water or as a glider

- Fixed or repositionable landing gear, or a hull, for an aircraft intended for operation on water

- Can be operated in day, VFR conditions only

In addition to understanding those characteristics typical of an LSA, it is also important to know what characteristics exclude an aircraft from this designation. These are:

- Part 103 ultralights – powered and unpowered hang gliders and paragliders

- Multi-engine aircraft

- Powered lift machines

- Helicopters

- Complex aircraft

- Aircraft previously certificated by the FAA, such as standard category aircraft (Luscombe 8A and Aeronca Champ) and experimental category aircraft such as the RV-4

Several different types of aircraft design can be covered by the LSA designation. The nature of low speed flight, which is more forgiving than high speed, allows for a wider variation in aircraft design. With that fact in mind, the FAA created rules for six types of aircraft:

- Fixed wing airplane

- Glider

- Powered parachute

- Lighter than air

- Weight shift control

- Gyroplane

Fixed wing airplane. The fixed wing airplane comprises the largest group of aircraft in the LSA definition. These aircraft range from heavy ultralights that have a conventional planform (wing, fuselage, tail) to modern composite designs that rival the most advanced aircraft available. Figures 1-1-1 and 1-1-2 represent the extreme ends of these designs. In addition to land aircraft, sea aircraft which are capable of landing on water are included in the rule; Figure 1-1-3 shows an example of an amphibious LSA with repositionable landing gear. The LSA rule does not allow aircraft with retractable landing gear for land use only, but does allow seaplanes

Figure 1-1-4. A production Schweitzer glider that meets the LSA definition.

to have a repositionable landing gear so that both land and sea operations are possible.

Glider. Gliders that meet the LSA rules include almost all sailplanes, both powered and unpowered, and a few manufacturers have marketed their aircraft directly to the LSA market. Like other fixed-wing LSA, these aircraft must have a V_{NE} of less than 120 kts. Gliders that meet the definition of LSA will include almost every sailplane currently available that has a V_{NE} of less than 120 kts. Since the weight limit is high for a sailplane (1,320 lbs), it is not anticipated that this will restrict any sailplanes currently available from qualifying as LSA. See Figure 1-1-4.

Powered parachute. After two and half years of development, the ParaPlane Corporation introduced the first fully functional aircraft at the 1983 Sun 'n' Fun Fly In at Lakeland, Florida. Today there are several manufacturers of powered parachutes that offer both ultralight designs and LSA designs. Figure 1-1-5 shows an example of one type of powered parachute.

Powered parachutes represent aircraft that are somewhere between balloons and fixed wing aircraft in their method of operation. Like a balloon they have no control surfaces; the direction of a powered parachute is altered by the pilot pushing on either a left or right foot pedal that in turn pulls down on a line attached to the trailing edge of the canopy, shown in Figure 1-1-6. The increased drag causes the aircraft to turn, and power must be added to maintain altitude. The foot pedals can also be used in unison, unlike conventional aircraft, which will droop both trailing ends of the canopy together and cause a sudden increase in lift. This maneuver, called flaring, is used to reduce the descent rate during landing; necessary if the engine has failed and the aircraft is descending at a typical 3:1 power-off glide ratio. Flaring the aircraft in such a manner should be performed close to the ground only, since airspeed will be bled off and a higher rate of descent will result after forward momentum is gone.

Figure 1-1-5. Powered parachutes feature a powered chassis suspended beneath a parachute.

Figure 1-1-6. When operating a powered parachute, pushing on either the left or right foot pedal controls the trailing edge of the canopy.

Due to the configuration and mounting of the canopy risers to the airframe, the canopy maintains a constant angle of attack regardless of the power setting used. Typical powered parachutes will climb, cruise and descend somewhere between 26 to 35 m.p.h., and cannot be flown at any other speed, unlike fixed wing aircraft. Not only are they *airspeed stable*, but due to the mass of the airframe suspended below the canopy, they are *pendulum stable* as well, This allows the aircraft to maintain a safe roll attitude and effectively turn in a coordinated manner when the steering pedals are deflected.

Figure 1-1-7. Backpack hot air balloon system

Lighter-than-air. Balloons and airships are currently the rarest of LSA, and few manufacturers have produced LSA-ready lighter-than-air aircraft. In order to meet the gross weight limit of 660 lbs., hot air balloons must be constructed of lightweight materials from the basket to the balloon envelope. The nature of hot-air ballooning lends itself to customization by the end user, so that trade-offs of fuel capacity, tank and frame construction, size of the envelope and the weight of the pilot can create an almost unlimited number of possible LSA designs. It remains to be seen if manufacturers will invest in LSA by offering these thin units as a lighter-than-air alternative. Figure 1-1-7 shows a typical backpack hot air balloon system.

Weight shift control. Weight shift control aircraft originate from the earliest hang glider designs where control is affected by the pilot moving his/her weight to change the aircraft center of gravity (CG). Otto Lilienthal built several gliders in the 1890s in Germany that established the first hang glider configuration, shown in Figure 1-1-8. The basic design of a hang glider today relies on the same elements that Lilienthal based his designs on: a wing structure, pilot suspension system, and an ability for the pilot to change their position by moving all or part of their body forward, aft, left and right. As the CG moves, the aircraft's attitude changes and this allows the pilot to control the flight path of the aircraft without the use of control surfaces.

Many of today's weight shift control aircraft have replaced the pilot with a pod that contains the propulsion system, seating for pilot and passenger, and usually three wheels that form the landing gear. It is the three-wheeled configuration of most of these weight shift aircraft that have resulted in them being referred to as trikes.

Figure 1-1-9 shows a typical trike configuration, with a triangular-shaped control bar extending down from the wing, which is gripped by the pilot and pushed or pulled to move the pod relative to the wing.

Gyroplane. The gyroplane has its roots in the autogiro, first designed by Juan de la Cierva in Spain in the 1920s. Several iterations of de la Cierva's initial concepts led to a functional autogiro design that incorporated a hinged (articulating) rotor, allowing the blades to rise and fall as the relative wind speed changed due to the forward speed of the aircraft. This novel idea solved the problem of asymmetrical lift on a rigid rotor, and allowed the autogiro to travel forward at speeds that rivaled fixed wing aircraft. Later in 1931, a cyclic control similar to that found on modern drum brake helicopters was demonstrated on autogiros and this became the first example of a successful rigid rotor design for these aircraft.

Pitcairn developed a very capable autogiro, designated the PCA-2, based on de la Cierva's work. Several PCA-2's were developed and were featured in the news by landing on the U.S. Capitol parking lot and transporting Senator Hiram Bingham to his golf games. As part of the demonstration of its capabilities, Amelia Earhart flew a PCA-2 to an altitude of

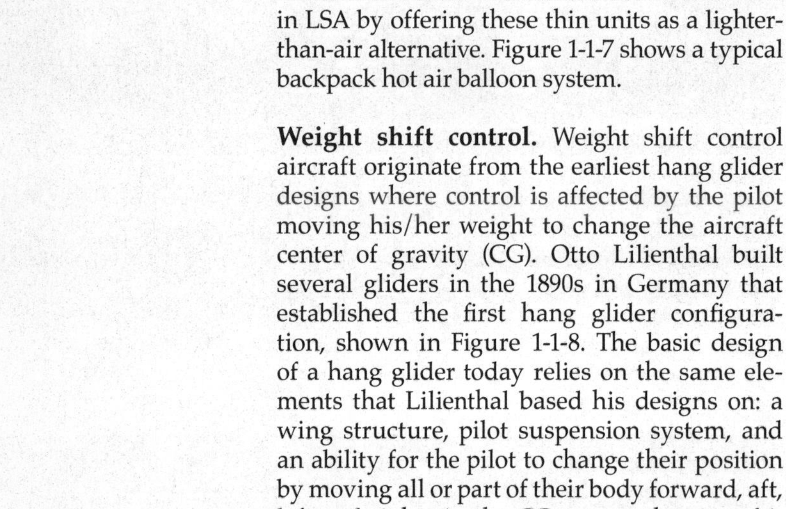

Figure 1-1-8. Lilienthal glider *Photo courtesy of Otto Lilienthal Museum, Anklam, Germany*

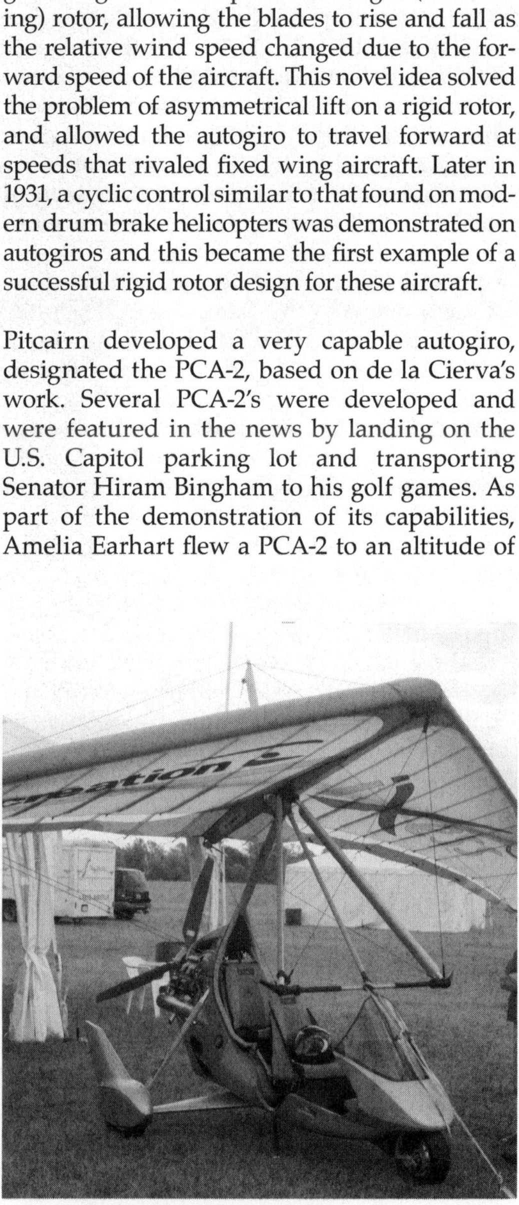

Figure 1-1-9. Trike configuration

18,415 feet, a record for 1931. The Pitcairn auto-giro is shown in Figure 1-1-10.

Gyroplanes, as they are referred to today, have been further developed over the years and a few models are currently available as LSA. One of de la Cierva's greatest contributions, the hinged rotor, can be seen in an LSA gyroplane in Figure 1-1-11. A common design for the modern gyro-plane is a pusher configuration with a conventional rudder and elevator that allows the pilot to control yaw and pitch, as shown in Figure 1-1-12. Due to roll/yaw coupling, these aircraft can effectively turn without ailerons, further simplifying their design and operation.

Figure 1-1-10. Pitcairn autogiro

Section 2

Light Sport Aircraft and Regulations Governing the Sport Pilot

The two major classifications of LSA certificates are *Special-Light Sport,* and *Experimental, Operating Light Sport.* The Special-Light Sport or S-LSA definition includes production aircraft that are maintained by certificated repairmen or mechanics. Experimental, Operating Light Sport Aircraft, or ELSA, are similar to amateur-built experimental aircraft in that the FAA does not regulate their maintenance.

Unlike amateur-built planes, ELSA have no minimum percentage of construction that must be performed by the owner. The owner/builder is only required to show that the finished construction of the aircraft was in accordance with

Figure 1-1-12. Gyroplane with a pusher configuration and conventional rudder.

applicable consensus standards and meets the definition of the light sport aircraft.

Differences between S-LSA and ELSA from an aircraft structures standpoint may be found only in the quality of assembly work performed by the owner as compared to that of the manufacturer. From a certification standpoint, there are several differences between the two aircraft, and these will be discussed next.

Table 1-2-1 (next page) outlines the certification requirements for pilots, mechanics and aircraft operating under LSA rules.

Transitioning ultralight-like aircraft to ELSA status. Ultralight-like aircraft can be certificated as ELSA after the owner accomplishes several required actions discussed in Chapter 2, and the aircraft is deemed safe and airworthy by the owner (as part of the airworthiness application). A

Figure 1-1-11. Hinged rotor on an LSA gyroplane

Designated Airworthiness Representative (DAR) will issue the ELSA certificate once a final inspection is completed. The FAA will allow ultralights to transition to ELSA until January 31, 2008. After that date, those aircraft that do not meet the requirements of FAR Part 103 but do meet the LSA requirements must be certificated directly as S-LSA or ELSA from the manufacturer.

Newly manufactured LSA. Newly manufactured LSA are either ready-to-fly or kit-built. The ready-to-fly aircraft, because they are produced by the manufacturer, are certificated as S-LSA. Kit-built aircraft, because they are ultimately assembled by the owner/operator are designated as ELSA. At this time, no manufacturer currently offers new kit-built aircraft, though as the industry matures, kits will become more readily available. See Figure 1-2-1. Purchasers of ready-to-fly S-LSA aircraft who fail to maintain and inspect the aircraft as required for S-LSA but meet the requirements for ELSA can apply for the experimental certificate and recertify their aircraft.

The owner/operator of a kit-built LSA does not have to meet the majority build rule that applies to amateur-built experimental aircraft, a rule that requires 51% of the aircraft to be constructed by the owner/homebuilder. The owner of an ELSA can be left with minor assembly required by the manufacturer; this will still allow the aircraft to be certificated as experimental. Consequently, the FAA has created new standards for experimental LSA inspections when compared to experimental amateur-built aircraft because the owner may not be deeply familiar with the construction of the aircraft. Recall that amateur built experimental aircraft can be inspected by the builder without having to complete any training in inspections. Requirements necessary to perform annual condition inspections on ELSA are discussed in Chapter 2.

Sport pilot privileges. Sport pilots are eligible to fly not only a variety of new-production LSA ranging from powered parachutes to fixed-wing aircraft, depending on their flight training and endorsements, but they may also fly other aircraft

LIGHT SPORT AIRCRAFT CERTIFICATION REQUIREMENTS					
ITEM	S-LSA			ELSA	
Pilot Certification	Instruction:	Airplane: Powered parachute: Weight shift control: Glider: Lighter-than-air (balloon):	15 hrs. 10 hrs. 15 hrs. 10 Flights 3 Flights	Logged flight time:	Airplane: Powered parachute: Weight shift control: Glider: Lighter-than-air: (airship) (balloon)	20 hrs. 12 20 10 20 7
	Testing:	Must pass an FAA sport pilot knowledge test Must pass an FAA sport pilot practical (flight) test				
	Must hold a current FAA medical or US driver's license. Must be at least 17 years of age (16 for glider or balloon)					
Aircraft Certification	Must meet provisions of FAA Order 8130.2F – Section 6			Must meet provisions of FAA Order 8130.2F – Section 8		
Annual Condition Inspection	Conducted per FAR § 91.327 and the operating limitations assigned by the FAA which can include FAR Part 43, Appendix D. Must be performed by a repairman with the maintenance rating, or an A & P with LSA experience, or a properly rated FAA repair station.			Conducted per operating limitations assigned by the FAA. Refer to FAR Part 43, Appendix D, "Scope and Detail of Items to be Included in Annual and 100-hour Inspections." Performed by rated persons as specified for S-LSA and includes repairmen with the inspection rating.		
Maintenance	Who: Repairman with the maintenance rating, or an A & P with LSA experience, or a properly rated FAA repair station. How: Performed in accordance with FAR Part 43 except for recording major repairs and alterations. Industry consensus standards are referenced. Safety directives from the manufacturer must be complied with. Airworthiness directives issued against FAA approved products must be complied with.			Who: Anyone can perform maintenance on an ELSA. How: Not regulated, but manufacturers will encourage owners to comply with consensus standards.		
Commercial Usage	Allowed and requires 100-hour inspections, similar to other commercial-use aircraft.			Allowed under special circumstances. Requires 100-hour inspections and does not allow aircraft leasing (except to pilots qualified for towing)		

Table 1-2-1. Certification requirements for pilots, mechanics and aircraft operating under LSA rules

that are not certified as LSA. These aircraft include previously certificated aircraft under the standard airworthiness category as well as those aircraft that are registered as experimental. The most common aircraft an LSA pilot will fly can be broken down into five types:

- Transitioning ultralight-like aircraft

- Newly manufactured LSA

- Kit-built LSA

- Amateur-built experimental aircraft meeting the definition of LSA

- Standard category production aircraft that meet the LSA definition, including common aircraft such as the Aeronca Champ and rag-wing Pipers.

Transitional ultralight-like aircraft. This includes any aircraft that has not been previously issued an airworthiness certificate, does not fall into the definition of an ultralight but does fall under the definition of an LSA. In the past, these aircraft were used as trainers in the ultralight world, where the pilot in command technically had to be giving instruction in order to carry a passenger on board. These training ultralights are exempt from meeting the FAR Part 103 definition of an ultralight, and because of this, they are much more capable in terms of range, speed and payload capacity.

Manufacturers have built and sold many of these aircraft over the years, and estimates currently in existence range from 8,000–15,000. The LSA rules will encompass these airplanes and the FAA has created a mechanism to bring these aircraft into the LSA community. More will be said about this in Chapter 2.

Pilots who can demonstrate flight experience and were registered with an organization recognized by the FAA such as Aero Sports Connection (ASC), Experimental Aircraft Association (EAA) and United States Ultralight Association (USUA) on or before September 1, 2004 are not required to log further flight instruction for the sport pilot license. These pilots must be at least 17 years of age and pass the knowledge and practical tests administered by the appropriate authorities. This process must be completed by January 31, 2007. Pilots registered after September 1, 2004 must show that they meet the minimum aeronautical experiences just as any other pilot applying for the LSA certificate would be required to do.

Newly manufactured or kit-built LSA. New production aircraft such as that shown in Figure 1-2-2 represent the core LSA business that promises to grow sport aviation to an untapped market. These aircraft are limited in performance by the LSA definition but show advances in aircraft construction that make

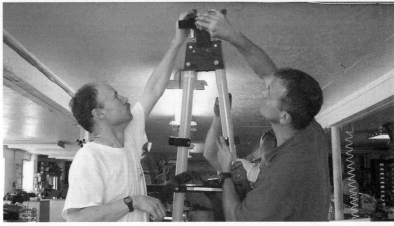

Figure 1-2-1. Kit-built aircraft may be designed with minimal or extensive assembly required by the owner.

Figure 1-2-2. This plane is one example of a newly manufactured LSA.

them safer and more economical to fly than typical general aviation aircraft. Pilots that fly these aircraft or any other aircraft that meet the LSA definition using a sport pilot certificate will have to comply with the privileges and limitations outlined in FAR Part 61.315. These include sharing flight expenses but not flying for compensation or hire, or furthering a business operation.

No more than one passenger can be carried, night and international flight is prohibited, flight into class A airspace is prohibited and flight into class B, C, and D airspace is restricted. Flight altitudes are limited to 10,000 feet MSL, visibility must be greater than 3 statute miles and visual reference to the surface must be maintained. Other limitations include ground and flight training and a logbook endorsement for operation at speeds greater than 87 knots CAS, and any other limitations that may be expressed by logbook endorsement.

Amateur-built experimental and standard category production aircraft. A sport pilot can fly any aircraft that meets the LSA definition even if that aircraft has been certificated under a different category. This allows many older aircraft that are relatively light and speed-limited to now become key players in the LSA community. The FAA has compiled a list of 131 aircraft that meet the LSA definition with most of them considered classic aircraft manufactured by companies such as Aeronca, Piper, Luscombe and Taylorcraft. This list can be found on the FAA website www.faa.gov, Regulatory Support Division, Light Sport Aviation Branch. These aircraft must still be inspected and maintained as required by their certification, and the pilot should be aware of the regulations governing standard category aircraft.

Similarly, many amateur-built experimental aircraft are also eligible for flight under the LSA rules, and it will be necessary to check with the FAA on a particular aircraft's eligibility.

> **NOTE:** *Experimental aircraft have additional operating limitations that must be complied with, such as restricted flight over congested areas.*

These are outlined in FAR Part 91.319, Aircraft Having Experimental Certificates: Operating Limitations.

As in the case of flying standard category aircraft, the pilot must be aware of the particular airworthiness requirements associated with the experimental certificate. Experimental aircraft must have an annual condition inspection performed by either the person who built the aircraft or an appropriately rated mechanic. The FAA defines an appropriately rated mechanic as one that has the airframe and powerplant ratings, commonly referred to as an A&P. Because of this, inspector qualifications for the experimental light sport aircraft are not applicable to amateur-built experimental aircraft.

> **NOTE:** *The 16-hour inspection course for experimental light sport aircraft does not apply to amateur-built experimental aircraft even if the aircraft meets the LSA definition.*

There has been much confusion about this in the past, and it is important to understand the difference between an amateur-built experimental and an experimental light sport aircraft.

Pilot Certification

The medical requirements for LSA pilots are unique in that a current U.S. driver's license may be used to fulfill the basic requirement, provided that any restrictions or limitations that are on the license be observed while operating an aircraft. In addition, the applicant for a Sport Pilot certificate must not have:

- Been denied the most recent application for an FAA medical certificate

- Had a medical certificate suspended or revoked

- Had the most recent authorization for a special issuance of a medical certificate withdrawn

Furthermore, when using a valid third class medical certificate or a current and valid US driver's license, the sport pilot must:

- Not know or have reason to know of any medical condition that would make the sport pilot certificate holder unable to operate a light sport aircraft in a safe manner.

Section 61.303 or §61.303 of the FARs addresses the operating limits and endorsement requirements that need to be met in order to operate a light sport aircraft. Principally, §61.303 outlines the above medical issues and shows what privileges are available depending on the specific FAA medical certificate held by the pilot.

As is the case for all FAA certificates, a sport pilot must have a logbook endorsement from an authorized instructor that has trained, reviewed or evaluated a study course over the elements in §61.309 and §61.311. A written knowledge test that covers the elements of §61.309 must be taken and passed as well as a practical test over those items in §61.311. Section 61.307 states the requirement for the knowledge and practical tests.

Some of the highlights, but by no means all of §61.309 are as follows:

- The applicable regulations of part 61 that relate to sport pilot privileges, limits, and flight operations must be known. The use of the applicable portions of the Aeronautical Information Manual (AIM) and FAA advisory circulars as they relate to sport pilots will be part of the knowledge requirements.

- To ensure proper navigation and pilotage the use of aeronautical charts for Visual Flight Rules (VFR) navigation using pilotage, dead reckoning, and navigation systems, must be well practiced.

- As is true for all VFR pilots, recognition of critical weather situations from the ground and in flight is essential; the effects of windshear and how to avoid it are a requirement as well.

- A pilot must know how to procure and use the aeronautical weather reports and forecasts which are part of the whole weather and navigation picture.

- Since a basic knowledge of the aircraft and its relationship to the atmosphere is needed, a good understanding of the effects of density altitude on takeoff and climb performance must be part of any instructional program.

- Due to the smaller size and responsiveness of the LSA to changes in weight and loading, the ability of the pilot to perform all weight and balance computations has to be tested.

- For any aircraft, regardless of the size or configuration the principles of aerodynamics, the awareness of stalls and their development into spins and spin recovery techniques are an essential part of the pilots basic knowledge.

- The different types of powerplants used on LSA as well as the various aircraft systems will need to be covered as well.

FAR part §61.309 covers a number of other elements that must be learned and should be referenced in detail when training to obtain a sport pilot certificate.

The practical portion of the certification that is covered under §61.311 contains the requirements for testing the ability of the prospective sport pilot to actually operate the aircraft in a safe and responsible manner. The following is a selection of the more important points in the section: See Figure 1-2-3.

- Preflight preparation

- Airport, seaplane base, and gliderport operations

- Takeoffs (or launches), landings, and go-arounds

- Performance maneuvers, and for gliders, performance speeds

- Ground reference maneuvers

- Navigation

- Slow flight

- Stalls

- Emergency operations

The FAA requires certain minimum hours of instruction and flight time for sport pilot certificate eligibility, shown in Table 1-2-1 and extracted from FAR Part 61.313. Not shown in the table are more specific requirements of cross-country flight time, solo flight operations and limitations on the period of time over which flights may occur. This section forms the basis for flight instruction and guides the flight instructor as to how much time is spent on each topic area. Section 61.87 discusses the specific skills that must be demonstrated prior to solo flight, such as the ability to fly basic climb, descent and turning maneuvers as well as takeoffs and landings in various conditions. These FARs should be carefully studied to not only get a big picture of flight training, but also to optimize the program for efficiency.

Figure 1-2-3. This LSA pilot is making some necessary preflight preparations.

As previously mentioned, individuals who have logged time as ultralight pilots and were registered with an FAA-recognized ultralight organization on or before September 1, 2004 are exempted from meeting the minimum flight time requirement. The pilot must still pass the knowledge and practical tests by January 31, 2007, otherwise the credited flight time will no longer apply and he or she will have to enter a basic flight training program as a beginning student.

When the knowledge and practical tests for a sport pilot certificate have been successfully passed, the FAA will issue a sport pilot certificate without any category and class of airplane indicated on the certificate. This will be handled with a logbook endorsement and will specifically list the make and model of aircraft the pilot is authorized to fly. This is different from other FAA-issued certificates which clearly show the category and class of aircraft a pilot is authorized to fly.

The process of obtaining the Sport Pilot certificate has been developed by the FAA in conjunction with practical applications based on methods that have been used successfully for many years. The hours of instruction and flight times are representative of minimum requirements and some people may take longer to master the skills and knowledge needed to embrace this dynamic area of aviation.

In summary, the sections of FAR 61 that pertain to the Sport Pilot are: §61.87, §61.89, §61.303, §61.307, §61.309, §61.311, §61.313, §61.315 - §61.327 and §61.329. The entire regulations that cover the Sport Pilot are available on the FAA's web pages. Those web pages represent the latest and most current information on all of the regulations that affect aviation and should be referenced at any time that there is a question of accuracy or interpretation.

Chapter 2

faa regulations

One of the concepts behind the light sport aircraft is found in the shift of the regulatory responsibility to the manufacturer through consensus standards, while the FAA keeps the enforcement responsibility. Because of this, the documentation and tracking of safety-of-flight issues no longer resides with the FAA and the manufacturer now has full responsibility for this area. All the standards regarding the design, operation and maintenance of LSA come from industry-based consensus standards, which the FAA has accepted. Since the FAA did not develop the standards, they have allowed the industry to take the lead on administering and regulating these standards. The standards in turn guide the FAA in developing its own regulations and procedures regarding the S-LSA and ELSA certifications. Much of what is stated in Order 8130.2F and the Federal Aviation Regulations (FAR) come directly from the consensus standards.

The original consensus standards can be downloaded from the American Society for Testing Materials (ASTM) website, www.astm.org, for a fee.

The regulations established by the FAA for LSA can be found through the FAA's website at www.faa.gov.

Learning Objectives:

- Light Sport Aircraft Certification
- Types of ELSA
- Annual Condition Inspections
- Maintenance of Light Sport Aircraft

Section 1

Light Sport Aircraft Certification

On November 5, 2004, the FAA identified S-LSA airworthiness certificate in Order 8130.2F. This certificate is further explained in FAR part 21 as a Special Airworthiness Certificate along with

Left: This T-Bird is an example of S-LSA which are gaining in popularity.

the other special certificates, such as Primary, Experimental and Restricted. The other type of certificate recognized by the FAA is the Standard Airworthiness Certificate that is issued to aircraft certificated in the Normal, Utility, Acrobatic and Transport categories, to mention a few. The standard certificate is most commonly issued to general aviation aircraft.

The hierarchy of category and class of aircraft recognized by the FAA is shown in Figure 2-1-1, a page from the application for airworthiness certificate. The Special-Light Sport Aircraft category, or S-LSA designation applies to factory-built light-sport aircraft that are ready to fly and are issued special airworthiness certificates under FAR part 21. These aircraft can be maintained and inspected by repairmen with a maintenance rating under FAR 65. This rating can be earned in a 120-hour course for airplane maintenance, or fewer hours for other types of aircraft, such as the powered parachute. For

this reason, the S-LSA is opening aviation to a completely new market of consumers and aviation service providers.

Another type of LSA is the Experimental Operating Light Sport, or ELSA, which has reduced airworthiness standards similar to other experimental aircraft. The reason for creating the ELSA option is to open LSA to a wider range of pilots and aircraft by reducing the cost of flying and to transition previously unregistered, non-ultralight aircraft into a legitimate FAA-recognized category. Pilot training requirements are identical for both S-LSA and ELSA, but the inspection and maintenance requirements have been greatly reduced. A 16-hour class in inspections will allow the owner of an ELSA to perform their own annual condition inspection. There is no FAA oversight regarding maintenance of an ELSA. As we will see in the following sections, the owner of an ELSA must provide more documentation to the FAA to certificate the aircraft compared to an S-LSA. This is because the ELSA owner must take on some of the duties that are a manufacturer's responsibility when certifying and producing aircraft.

The specific parts of Order 8130.2F that apply to LSA are in Chapter 4: Special Airworthiness Certification. They are as follows:

- Section 1: General Information

- Section 6: Light-Sport Category Aircraft Airworthiness Certifications

- Section 8: Experimental Light-Sport Aircraft Airworthiness Certifications

The complete Order may be downloaded from the FAA website and should be used as a final reference in all matters concerning interpretation. The Federal Aviation Regulations that are referenced can be found on the same website.

General Information

Chapter 4, Section 1 of Order 8130.2F applies to all applicants for an airworthiness certificate, specifically manufacturers and experimental aircraft owners. Sections 1 and 6 are for manufacturers of S-LSA and Sections 1 and 8 are for owners of ELSA. Included in Section 1 are the steps the FAA takes in the certification process.

As is the case with any aircraft that is being inspected, the forms and records are the beginning of the inspection.

There are certain documents that will be requested by the FAA that are part of the certification file for the aircraft. These must be properly prepared and submitted at the time of the FAA inspection. Among those are the appli-

FAA FORM 8130-6, APPLICATION FOR U.S. AIRWORTHINESS CERTIFICATE

Figure 2-1-1. Page from airworthiness certificate application, Form 8130-6

cation for the airworthiness certificate, Form 8130-6 (Figure 2-1-1), a letter from the applicant that identifies the aircraft, the purpose of the certificate and the flight test area that will be over flown during that period of testing. The FAA will also verify if a denial letter has ever been issued for that particular aircraft.

The aircraft records and technical information that will be reviewed include the aircraft records for completeness of maintenance entries, alterations, and AD compliance. The weight and balance information must be current and apply to the aircraft being inspected. Any technical data needed to establish conformity to type design, and other documentation as required by certain airworthiness parts of the FARs will need to be presented as well. The registration requirements of FAR part 47 and part 45 will be reviewed, and the FAA will make sure that all the markings are in accordance with the requirements of the regulations. In the event that the aircraft has never flown, the FAA will issue Phase 1 Limitations, which restrict aircraft operations to certain geographical areas and flight conditions until the aircraft has been proven airworthy and safe.

Aircraft inspection. The FAA must arrange with the applicant to make the aircraft available for inspection to determine the following:

The physical inspection of the aircraft will follow the review of the documents that pertain to the aircraft. The aircraft is checked against the applicable Type Certificate Data Sheets (TCDS), Aircraft Specifications or Aircraft Listing to make sure that the aircraft is eligible for the designation sought. The next step is to verify that the information on the ID plate matches what is on Form 8130-6 and complies with FAR part 45. This includes the nationality and registration markings (N number) on the side of the aircraft. The instrument markings will be in agreement with the information in the flight manual or any other data used in the certification program.

The flight control systems must operate properly, as should the engine and propeller. The pitot static system and associated instruments will be inspected and checked as well. Should an Emergency Locator Transmitter be required, its installation will be inspected by the FAA. If any modifications to the aircraft were made, then they will be inspected and the proper documentation will be part of the FAA's inspection.

Special Light-Sport Category Aircraft Airworthiness Certifications

Chapter 4, section 6 of the Order spells out in detail what is required of the manufacturer to certificate an aircraft as an S-LSA, supplementary to the requirements of Section 1. In the interest of knowing the steps that the manufacturer must take to certify an aircraft design, a short overview of FAR part 21, as it applies to the S-LSA is included.

The issuance of a special airworthiness certificate for a light sport aircraft occurs when the manufacturer provides to the FAA a set of documents that contain the aircraft's operating instructions, maintenance and inspection procedures as well as the flight training supplements. A statement of compliance by the manufacturer must contain the make, model, serial numbers, and class of aircraft that are being certificated. All the consensus standards that are used to manufacture the aircraft have to be referenced. A system to correct safety-of-flight items must be established by the manufacturer, where the owner will be notified of any safety defects or faults. This is the basis of the safety directive system and takes the place of the Airworthiness Directive system used by the FAA. There are provisions in FAR part 21 for aircraft that are manufactured outside of the United States and

11/5/2004   8130.2F

FIGURE 2-3. SAMPLE LIMITATIONS FOR THE OPERATION OF AN AIRCRAFT WITH A DOOR REMOVED

U.S. Department
of Transportation
**Federal Aviation
Administration**

Make _____
Model _____ Serial No._____
Registration No. _____

AIRCRAFT OPERATING LIMITATIONS

The aircraft described above may be flown with not more than one cabin door removed for the purpose of (see note below), provided the aircraft is operated in accordance with the applicable sections of 14 CFR and the following limitations:

Note: Show specific operations; for example, intentional parachute jumping, skydiving, etc.

1.   Maximum speed not to exceed any of the following:

The approved maneuvering speed.
70 percent maximum level flight speed.
70 percent maximum structural cruising speed.

2.   Aerobatic maneuvers are not permitted.

3.   Maximum yaw angle 10 degrees; maximum bank angle 15 degrees.

4.   An FAA-approved safety belt must be provided and worn by each occupant during takeoff and landing and at all other times when required by the pilot-in-command.

5.   All occupants must wear parachutes when intentional parachute jumping and skydiving operations are conducted.

6.   Smoking is not permitted.

7.   When operations other than intentional parachute jumping and skydiving are conducted, a suitable guardrail or equivalent safety device must be provided for the doorway.

8.   All loose articles must be tied down or stowed.

9.   No baggage may be carried.

Page 37

Figure 2-1-2. A sample set of operating limitations

Figure 2-2-1. An example of a transitional ultralight

the proper certification procedures for those aircraft. Additionally, the test flight data and aircraft performance information must be presented to the FAA. In all, the certification package is a document that contains a detailed summary of the methods used to manufacture and test the aircraft, prior to its being granted an airworthiness certificate.

Upon satisfactory completion of these items and the others listed in the Order, the FAA issues the special airworthiness certificate and operating limitations for that aircraft. The operating limitations will be attached to the airworthiness certificate, Form 8130-7. The concept of operating limitations issued by the FAA unique to each aircraft has traditionally been associated with amateur-built, experimental aircraft. The FAA has adopted this model for all LSA aircraft, applying it to both S-LSA and ELSA. A typical set of operating limitations is shown in Figure 2-1-2 (previous page).

It should be emphasized that the purchaser of an S-LSA is not responsible for the above items; these will be taken care of by the manufacturer or aircraft dealer. Like other certificated aircraft, however, the owner will be responsible for ensuring that the aircraft is maintained and inspected to a standard enforced by the FAA. Unique to other certificated aircraft, however, is the fact that these standards were developed by the industry through the ASTM, as mentioned previously (consensus standards). This is truly revolutionary, whereas in the past, all aspects of aircraft design, production, quality control, etc. would be determined and governed by the FAA. For these types of aircraft, the FAA has turned over the development of the standards to the industry, while they are still maintaining enforcement authority.

The best example of this can be found in comparing Airworthiness Directives (AD) to Safety Directives (SD). For standard-certificated aircraft, ADs are generated for an aircraft or an approved aircraft component when the FAA

determines that a safety-of-flight issue exists based on data they have collected. The FAA will issue the AD to aircraft owners of record, and it is the responsibility of the owner to see that it is complied with in accordance with the compliance section of the AD. In the case of LSA, safety directives are generated by the manufacturer when they have compiled data indicating a safety-of-flight issue exists, and it is the manufacturer's responsibility to notify the aircraft owners or record of the situation.

The FAA maintains enforcement authority through FAR part 91, which states, "The owner or operator complies with each safety directive applicable to the aircraft that corrects an existing unsafe condition."

As a way of relaxing some of the burden on the owner to maintain and inspect their aircraft, the FAA has created the ELSA option for sport pilots. Similar to amateur-built experimental aircraft, the owner becomes the responsible party in determining how the aircraft is maintained. The owner must have a repairman's certificate with the inspection rating to perform annual condition inspections, but the decision to implement safety directives or method of compliance with rests entirely with the owner. As will be shown in the next section, the trade-off between S-LSA and ELSA will be found in an increased amount of work to certificate the aircraft.

Experimental Light Sport Aircraft Airworthiness Certifications

If the LSA owner plans to take the experimental route and purchase an aircraft designated as an Experimental–Operating Light Sport, the owner must accomplish some of the tasks that were previously part of the manufacturer's requirements to certificate an S-LSA. For airplanes that are Experimental, the FAA recognizes several purposes, including Amateur-built, and Operating Light Sport. The Special Experimental, Operating Light Sport Aircraft, or ELSA, is the other type of LSA addressed in Order 8130.2F, Chapter 4, sections 1 and 8 specifically address this.

This aircraft is issued an experimental certificate under FAR part 21. As an experimental aircraft, the pilot training requirements are the same as for S-LSA, but the maintenance and inspection requirements are reduced from S-LSA. The owner can perform inspections on their own aircraft after completing a 16-hour course specific to the type of aircraft they own. Maintenance on ELSA can be performed by the owner without a certificate, just as with amateur-built, experimental aircraft.

Section 2

Types of ELSA

Transitional Ultralight-like Aircraft

These are aircraft fabricated, assembled or manufactured before September 1, 2004 and are grandfathered by exception to the rule. These aircraft do not have to meet the requirements of the consensus standards for manufacture, however they must be in a condition for safe operation as demonstrated by a history of flights, or a series of test flights as recorded in the aircraft logbook. These aircraft must not have been issued any type of airworthiness certificate and they must not meet the provisions of FAR part 103 as an ultralight. Finally, they will not be issued an experimental certificate after January 31, 2008.

The first type of LSA is commonly referred to as the transitional ultralight, since these aircraft are frequently flown under ultralight rules even though they do not qualify as ultralights. The rules governing ultralight aircraft are contained in FAR part 103 and describe an ultralight. The description is specific about weight and speeds, both in level flight and stall speeds. The weights for these transitional aircraft, if they are powered, are below 254 pounds, empty excluding floats and safety devices. If unpowered, they must weigh less than 155 pounds. Both the powered and unpowered aircraft can only have a single occupant and they must be used for recreation or sport flying. The speeds for these aircraft are low when compared to other aircraft. At full power in level flight, the top speed cannot be more than 55 knots, cali-

brated airspeed, and a power off stall speed of 24 knots calibrated airspeed. Lastly, they are limited to a fuel load of only five US gallons. There is an exception to this rule when the aircraft is to be used for flight instruction or towing. See Figure 2-2-1.

The FAA is allowing previously unregistered aircraft flown as heavy ultralights to be newly registered as ELSA provided the owner applies for and receives an airworthiness certificate no later than January 31, 2008. While the other types of ELSA must be designed to a consensus standard, the transitional planes only have to demonstrate that they are in a condition for safe operation. The airworthiness certificate issued in this case has an unlimited duration, except when the aircraft is used for flight instruction or towing. For these limited commercial purposes, the airworthiness certificate will expire on January 31, 2010. The owner can apply for a recurrent experimental certificate of unlimited duration when the aircraft is no longer used for flight training or towing. If the instructor still wishes to flight instruct or tow, they must use an S-LSA for that purpose beyond the cut-off date.

The process of bringing a transitional airplane to ELSA-legal status may have little to do with the design of the aircraft, but it has a lot to do with its documentation. The Order 8130.2F Chapter 4, Section 1 contains the Certification Procedure items which must be addressed by the owner before an airworthiness certificate can be issued. The FAA or a Designated Airworthiness Representative (DAR) will inspect and review the following items:

Record inspection and document review. The FAA must inspect:

- Form 8130-6
- Letter describing the aircraft and its purpose
- Form 8130-15 Statement of Compliance
- Review FAR 45 and 47 for markings and registration
- Aircraft records and AD lists
- Weight and balance data

Aircraft inspection. The applicant must arrange with the FAA and/or DAR to make the aircraft available for inspection. The inspector will verify that the ID plate meets the requirements of FAR part 45: it must be fireproof; permanently affixed to the aircraft or engine; located as specified by the regulation on the engine, airframe or balloon; the information on the ID plate is correct, matches the information on Form 8130-6, and has at least the following:

- Builder's name

Figure 2-2-2. The Kappa KP-5 may be offered as a kit in the future

- Model designation
- Builder's serial number
- Type certificate number, if any
- Production certificate number, if any

Additionally, the following items will be inspected by the FAA as outlined in this order:

- The aircraft nationality and registration marks are in accordance with FAR §45, as applicable:
- The flight control systems and associated instruments, as equipped, operate properly and are appropriate for each of the six classes of LSA.
- The cockpit instruments are appropriately marked, and placards are installed and placed for easy reference.
- System controls (for example, fuel selector(s) and electrical switches/breakers) are appropriately placed, clearly marked, provide easy access and operation, and function in accordance with the manufacturer's specifications and applicable consensus standard.
- An ELT is installed, when required
- All pyrotechnic devices used in ballistic parachutes are clearly marked and identified.

While the FAA is involved in the inspection and certification that is required by the Order, the requirements of FAR 21 must also be satisfied. A number of the items listed in the FAR are actually the same as those in the Order, with some modifcations. A set of documents that contain statements about the use of the aircraft, as well as a set of photographs and or drawings that can be used to identify the aircraft and any information that is needed to safeguard the public must be submitted for review. In the case of a kit-built aircraft that is to be certificated, the applicant must provide evidence that aircraft of the same make, model have been manufactured, assembled and been granted an airworthiness certificate. The aircraft operating instructions, maintenance requirements and inspections must be included.

It is the FAA's responsibility to ensure that the aircraft submitted for certification complies with the items found in Sections 1 and 8 of the Order and the applicable FARs. The owner of a transitional ultralight should also plan on writing to the FAA requesting a registration number (N number) for a first-time registration. Included in the letter should be a completed Form 8050-1, Aircraft Registration Application, a completed Form 8050-2, Aircraft Bill of Sale, or Form 8050-88A, Affidavit of Ownership, whichever is applicable. The FAA will assign a registration number unless a custom registration number has been requested.

Aircraft marks with the Roman capital letter N (denoting United States registration) followed by the registration number of the aircraft must be displayed per FAR §45. Also near each entrance to the cabin, cockpit, or pilot station, in letters not less than 2 inches nor more than 6 inches high, the words limited, restricted, light-sport, experimental, or provisional, as applicable must be displayed.

An aircraft ready for experimental certification will contain a Form 8050-3 Aircraft Registration and an up-to-date weight and balance. The weight and balance on an ELSA differs from the weight and balance envelope commonly associated with FAR Part 23 certificated aircraft (general aviation) in that significant detail can be missing. For example, a powered parachute weight and balance data sheet may refer to the gross weight at "most critical CG location," but not actually identify where the CG is.

The applicant will attest that the aircraft has been inspected and is in an airworthy condition by signing Form 8130-6, the application for airworthiness. It is important to point out that the applicant does not need any training or certification to make this statement; it merely allows the DAR to proceed with their inspection assuming the aircraft is airworthy.

In order to assist transitional ultralight owners in the certification process, the Experimental Aircraft Association (EAA) has published a kit that guides owners through the certification process. The kit is easy to follow, and provides important items such as a blank identification plate for the aircraft, a decal designating the aircraft as experimental and various placards designed for the cockpit. This kit may be obtained through EAA member services, phone number 800-JOIN-EAA.

Light Sport Kit Aircraft or Kit-built LSA

These are aircraft kits sold by LSA manufacturers based on certificated S-LSA designs. They are constructed in accordance with the assembly instructions as outlined in the applicable consensus standards.

Since LSA manufacturers have concentrated on building ready-to-fly aircraft and meeting the consensus standards for production aircraft, there has been little interest in producing ELSA kits. Existing amateur-built aircraft cannot be transitioned to ELSA, even though they may appear to be identical to an ELSA kit plane. This is prohibited by FAR part 21 since an eligible aircraft cannot be previously certificated in another category. It is expected that the market for kit-built ELSA will increase as the sport matures, but for now it remains a small interest. See Figure 2-2-2.

When the origin of an ELSA is from a kit provided by the LSA manufacturer, the applicant for the ELSA certificate must show that the aircraft was manufactured and assembled to the applicable consensus standard. It will be necessary for the builder of the ELSA to obtain pertinent documentation from the manufacturer, which shows that the finished aircraft meets the criteria in FAR part 21 and that all applicable documents and records are properly filled out. Some of the important document contents are the statements by the manufacturer concerning compliance with the applicable consensus standards, and quality assurance standards that have been used to manufacture the aircraft. The flight test data must also be included in the documentation associated with the aircraft.

The Order 8130.2F additionally states that, "the LSA kit does not have to meet a major portion requirement and the applicant does not have to show the FAA that completion of the aircraft is not an assembly operation only." This is different from Experimental, Amateur-built aircraft that require the builder to show that they completed a majority (51%) of the construction themselves.

In addition to complying with FAR part 21, the Certification Procedures from the Order and previously listed for transitional ultralights apply to kit-built aircraft as well.

While the owner must provide more information to the FAA under FAR part 21 for a kit-built ELSA as opposed to an S-LSA, many items found in the Order will already be taken care of by the manufacturer, such as the marking of the aircraft and installation of required items such as an ELT. These aircraft may require more flight-testing than the transitional ultralight since they are new and have not logged any flight time. The baseline time for phase I flight-testing is established by the FAA, and the inspector will work with the owner to define an acceptable geographic area where the flight-testing may occur. Aircraft operations are limited to the flight test area until the aircraft is shown to be controllable throughout its normal range of speeds and maneuvers and has not displayed any hazardous operating characteristics or design features.

The owner inspection, required for the completion of the Airworthiness Certificate Application Form 8130-6, will be performed in accordance with the applicable consensus standard and provided by the manufacturer. For this inspection, the builder's signature attests to the airworthiness of the experimental LSA. Like the transitional aircraft, the builder does not need to possess the Repairman's Certificate to perform this inspection prior to the FAA's inspection.

Previously Certificated Special LSA Aircraft

These are aircraft that have been previously flight tested and are not required to have any additional flight-testing, unless they have been altered. The alterations must have been recorded in the aircraft logbooks before the original certification. These aircraft are "downgraded" from S-LSA to ELSA status.

The most interesting method of obtaining an ELSA is to start with an S-LSA, and re-certificate it as an ELSA, when the owner has decided not to keep up with the S-LSA standards. In doing so, the owner will follow the methods outlined in Section 8 of the Order, but since the aircraft has presumably already flown several hours, there will be no phase I flight testing. The exception is when the owner has modified the aircraft in some manner, resulting in essentially a new experimental aircraft that must be test flown under phase I to prove its controllability throughout the normal range of speeds. See Figure 2-2-3.

Figure 2-2-3. CT during phase I test flight.   *Photo courtesy of Flight Design USA*

The owner will be required to produce all other documentation outlined in the Order for experimental aircraft certification, with the exception of complying with the kit-built consensus standards (since the aircraft was factory built). Owners should be aware that in letting an S-LSA convert to an ELSA may lower the resale value.

To summarize the conversion process, the owner of an S-LSA wishing to convert to ELSA will:

- Contact an FAA inspector or DAR to meet for an inspection of the documents and aircraft

- Surrender the S-LSA airworthiness certificate

- Submit a completed Form 8130-6 with the Experimental, Operating Light Sport, and Operating light sport previously issued special light sport category airworthiness certificate under §21.190 boxes checked

- Submit all data as requested in FAR part 21

Since the aircraft was already certificated, placards and markings are probably complete. The owner will still have to produce items for the Record Inspection and Document Review, as listed in the Order.

Light Sport Operating Limitations

In general, the FAA has defined the operating limitations on experimental aircraft in FAR part 91. This rule states that no person may operate an aircraft that has an experimental certificate:

- For hire or compensation, unless specifically exempt

- The aircraft is shown to be safe through its normal range of speeds and maneuvers

- Over densely populated areas, unless specifically exempt

- For towing of gliders or un-powered ultra-lights

In addition, each person that is operating an aircraft with an experimental certificate shall:

- Advise any person carried of the experimental nature of the aircraft

- Operate under day VFR conditions, unless specifically exempt

- Notify the control tower of the experimental nature of the aircraft, when applicable

As part of the airworthiness certificate that is issued to an ELSA, the FAA includes a list of operating limitations, which are tailored to the particular aircraft and certificate that the FAA is issuing. Not only are operating limitations part of the experimental certificate, as they have been in the past for amateur-built aircraft, but the FAA is also issuing operating limitations on S-LSA aircraft as well (mentioned previoiously). The benefit of this type of regulatory process is that the wide range of LSA designs can be evaluated and only those restrictions applicable to a particular design are enforced.

Once the records, documents and inspections, as outlined in the Order, have been completed satisfactorily, the FAA will issues a Form 8130-7, Special Airworthiness Certificate with the operating limitations attached to the certificate. This certificate will be displayed in the cockpit of the aircraft per FAR part 91, "…at the cabin or cockpit entrance so that it is legible to passengers and crew." To appreciate what operating limitations may appear on the S-LSA and ELSA certificates, Table 2-2-1 summarizes several of the limitations found in the Order. This is not a complete list, and reference should be made to the Order for the full details including which limitations are mandatory and which can be optionally assigned by the FAA/DAR in a particular situation.

Section 3

Annual Condition Inspections

Annual condition inspections (once every 12 calendar months) are required of both S-LSA and ELSA to ensure that the aircraft are airworthy, but the similarity abruptly ends there. For S-LSA, the inspection is required per FAR part 91 General Operating and Flight Rules. This FAR states that the condition inspection is to be "in accordance with inspection procedures developed by the aircraft manufacturer or a person acceptable to the FAA". Therefore, the standards by which the condition inspection is conducted for S – LSA will be specific to each airplane. In the event that the aircraft is used for compensation or hire the FAA will require 100 hour inspection similar to other aircraft used for commercial purposes.

It should be noted here that the procedures for the condition inspection developed by the aircraft manufacturer are in accordance with the ASTM consensus standards, standard F2483-05, (Standard Practice for Maintenance) in particular. This standard ensures some uniformity in the format and content of an inspection checklist, so variations from aircraft to aircraft should be minimal. The consensus standards define a new term in the maintenance and inspection vocabulary: Safety Directive or SD. This was previously mentioned as the LSA equivalent of an AD issued against standard certificated aircraft, where a safety-of-flight issue must be addressed by the aircraft owner/operator. The SD is issued by the aircraft manufacturer and not the FAA, so the manufacturer is responsible for tracking, evaluating and issuing the SD based on data it collects. The FAA is only involved from an enforcement standpoint, since the FARs specifically prohibit the operation of an aircraft that has known safety problems. For S-LSA, the condition inspection will include a review of the SDs issued against the aircraft, and a determination will be made if they have been complied with before the aircraft is considered airworthy.

The adherence to safety directives applies only to S-LSA and not ELSA, however inspections of any LSA should include a review of the SDs for applicability and compliance. The annual condition inspection for an S-LSA is required in FAR part 91, whereas no FAR specifies an annual condition inspection for ELSA. Part 43 states: "Each person performing an inspection required by the applicable parts of the FARS Part 91, 123, 125, or 135 of this chapter, shall...perform the inspection so as to determine whether the aircraft, or portion(s) thereof under inspection, meets all applicable airworthiness requirements" again this applies only to S-LSA aircraft.

The person performing the annual condition inspection on an S-LSA must possess at least a Repairman's Certificate with the maintenance rating, issued under FAR part 65, and eligibility can be can be determined from Table 3-3-1 (next page). That person will complete an 80 to 120 hour course in LSA maintenance depending on the class of LSA for which the rating applies. For instance, a rating to perform maintenance on a fixed-wing LSA will require completion of a 120 hours course. Gliders only require 80 hours of instruction. The holder will be able to use this certificate for commercial purposes.

If an airframe and powerplant mechanic (A & P) performs the annual condition inspection, they must show previous experience with LSA. Airframe and Powerplant mechanics (A&Ps) who can show either that they worked on an LSA before, were trained to work on LSA, or were supervised by a mechanic or repairman with LSA experience perform the condition inspection. Furthermore, a rated repair station may also perform the inspection provided proper inspection procedures are used.

Unlike S-LSA, the annual condition inspection for the ELSA will be specified in the operating limitations assigned to the aircraft by the FAA as part of the airworthiness certificate. This is

OPERATING LIMITATION	AIRCRAFT	DESCRIPTION
Piloted Operations	LSA and ELSA	Aircraft operation is restricted to either experimental-operating LSA or special-LSA
Pilot Certification	LSA and ELSA	Pilot in command holds light sport pilot certificate
Phase 1 Flight Testing	ELSA	Flights are restricted to a geographic location
Phase 1 Flight Testing	ELSA	Flights restricted to an area for ____ hours
Phase 1 Flight Testing	LSA and ELSA	Must be conducted in VFR, day only conditions
Flight Testing	LSA and ELSA	No person may be carried unless essential for flight
Commercial Operation	ELSA	Allowed for towing and flight instruction under exemption with 100-hour or 12-month inspections
Commercial Operation	LSA	Allowed with a 100-hour or 12-month inspection
Commercial Operation	LSA	Prohibited except for flight instruction and towing
Flight Operations	LSA and ELSA	Aircraft must be operated in accordance with operating limitations, carried in the aircraft
Aerobatics	ELSA	Aerobatic flight is prohibited
Aerobatics	ELSA	Aerobatic flight is allowed
Passengers	LSA and ELSA	Must be briefed on the nature of the aircraft
Night Flying	LSA and ELSA	Unless equipped for night and/or instrument flying in accordance to § 91.205, this aircraft must be flown VFR, day only
Night Flying	LSA and ELSA	Aircraft instruments and equipment installed and used under § 91.205 must be inspected and maintained according to part 91. Maintenance or inspection must be recorded in aircraft records
Placards	LSA and ELSA	Placards and markings as required by § 91.9 must be installed and inspected for legibility and clarity
Condition Inspection	LSA and ELSA	Aircraft must complete a condition inspection within preceding 12 months in accordance with App. D, part 43
Condition Inspection	ELSA	An ELSA owner/operator may perform inspections under § 65.107
Condition Inspection	ELSA	Must be recorded with appropriately worded statement: "I certify that this aircraft has been inspected on [insert date] in accordance with the scope and detail to appendix D to part 43, and was found to be in a condition for safe operation"
Flight Instruction and Towing	Transitional ELSA	Allowed by exemption until January 31, 2010

Table 2-2-1. Operating limitations for light sport aircraft.

TO BE ELIGIBLE FOR	YOU MUST
A repairman certificate (light-sport aircraft)	(i) Be at least 18 years old. (ii) Be able to read, speak, write, and understand English. If for medical reasons you cannot meet one of these requirements, the FAA may place limits on your repairman certificate necessary to safely perform the actions authorized by the certificate and rating. (iii) Demonstrate the requisite skill to determine whether a light-sport aircraft is in a condition for safe operation, and (iv) Be a citizen of the United States, or a citizen of a foreign country who has been lawfully admitted for permanent residence in the United States.
A repairman certificate (light-sport aircraft) with an inspection rating	(i) Be at least 18 years old. (ii) Be able to read, speak, write, and understand English. If for medical reasons you cannot meet one of these requirements, the FAA may place limits on your repairman certificate necessary to safely perform the actions authorized by the certificate and rating.
A repairman certificate (light-sport aircraft) with a maintenance rating	(i) Meet the requirements of paragraph (1) of this section, and (ii) Complete a training course acceptable to the FAA on maintain the particular class of light-sport aircraft for which you intend to exercise the privileges of this rating. The training course must, at a minimum, provide the following number of hours of instruction: (A) For airplane class privileges—120 hours. (B) For weight-shift control aircraft class privileges—104 hours. (C) For powered parachute class privileges—104 hours. (D) For lighter than air class privileges—80 hours. (E) For glider class privileges—80 hours.

Table 2-3-1. Basic requirements for a repairman certificate

because there is no specific FAR requiring a condition inspection on an experimental aircraft. In the list of possible operating limitations published in Order 8130.2F, the FAA's wording that governs the condition inspection only refers to Appendix D of FAR part 43, and does not refer to the consensus standards or the manufacturer's provided checklists for the annual or 100-hour inspections. It is in the best interest of the owner to use the available information on inspections that the manufacturer can provide, but again, it is not mandatory. The two operating limitations for ELSA pertaining to annual condition inspections that will always be listed with the airworthiness certificate are:

- No person may operate this aircraft unless within the preceding 12 calendar months it has had a condition inspection performed in accordance with the scope and detail to Appendix D to part 43, or other FAA-approved programs, and was found to be in a condition for safe operation. As part of the condition inspection, cockpit instruments must be appropriately marked and needed placards installed in accordance with § 91.9. In addition, system-essential controls must be in good condition, securely mounted, clearly marked, and provide for ease of operation. This inspection will be recorded in the aircraft maintenance records.

- Condition inspections must be recorded in the aircraft maintenance records showing the following (or a similarly worded) statement: "I certify that this aircraft has been inspected on [insert date] in accordance with the scope and detail of appendix D to part 43, and was found to be in a condition for safe operation. The entry will include the aircraft's total time-in-service, and the name, signature, certificate number, and type of certificate held by the person performing the inspection.

Appendix D of FAR part 43 is a broad overview of the items that should be inspected during an annual or 100-hour inspection. Since this appendix was written to apply to all aircraft, it is very generic and allows considerable latitude as to the depth of the inspection. It is also the minimum requirement for any checklist since many manufactures will have items that must be inspected in greater detail. A complete text of Appendix D can be found at www.faa.gov.

The person performing an inspection on an ELSA can be the owner who possesses the Repairman's Certificate with the Inspection Rating as defined in FAR part 65. This certificate is earned in a 16-hour course designed around a 75% lecture, 25% hands-on format. There are six possible specializations (classes for aircraft) in this course:

- Airplane

- Powered parachute

- Weight shift control

- Gyroplane

- Lighter than air

- Glider

Table 2-3-1 lists the basic requirements for a repairman certificate.

The course completion certificate will acknowledge the class of aircraft and the hours of instruction. With this certificate and proof-of-ownership of the aircraft, the applicant can request from the FAA the Repairman's Certificate with Inspection rating that is specific to the aircraft owned by the certificate holder.

Section 4

Maintenance of Light Sport Aircraft

Similar to the inspection procedures, S-LSA maintenance is governed by the FARs, and in particular, FAR part 91 which states that the aircraft be maintained by a person with the appropriate certificate and the applicable provisions of FAR part 43.

The applicable provisions of part 43 state that the entire part 43 applies to S-LSA except for certain portions, pertaining to major repairs and major alterations. In stating these exceptions to part 43, the FAA has eliminated the need to document certain maintenance items (major repairs and alterations) that, before S-LSA, were regulated by the FAA. Since all maintenance will be regulated by the consensus standards through the manufacturer, there is no need for a paper trail to be left with the FAA; the manufacturers will take on that responsibility. The entire FAR 43 may be downloaded from the FAA web site and should be used whenever there is a question of interpretation or content.

Remember, all standards regarding the design, operation and maintenance of LSA come from industry-based consensus standards, which the FAA has accepted. Since the FAA did not develop the standards, they have allowed the industry to take the lead on administering and regulating these standards.

Those who can perform maintenance on an S-LSA are similar to those that can inspect an S-LSA: they must possess at least a Repairman Certificate with the Maintenance Rating, as defined in FAR part 65. As previously mentioned, this is after a course that specializes in a particular type of LSA, such as airplane, powered parachute, weight shift control, lighter than air, or glider. An A&P who can show that they either; worked on an LSA before, were trained to work on LSA, or were supervised by a mechanic or repairman with experience on LSAs, can also perform the condition inspec-

tion as well as the maintenance. FAR part 65 gives that maintenance authority to a certificated mechanic. See Figure 2-4-1.

The FAA has made maintenance on an LSA easier (and cheaper) by reducing the paperwork and oversight of the mechanic, but the trade-off is that the owner must assume the added responsibility as defined by the consensus standards. Standard F2295-03, Continued Operational Safety Monitoring of a Light Sport Airplane, lists several owner/operator responsibilities:

- Comply with maintenance and continued airworthiness information provided by the manufacturer.

- Provide the manufacturer with current contact information for the owner/operator.

- The owner/operator shall be responsible for notifying the manufacturer of any safety of flight issue.

- The owner/operator is responsible for complying with all manufacturer-issued notices of corrective action and for complying with all applicable aviation authority regulations in regard to maintaining the airworthiness of the LSA airplane.

- An owner of an LSA airplane shall ensure that any needed corrective action be completed as specified in a notice, or by the next scheduled annual inspection.

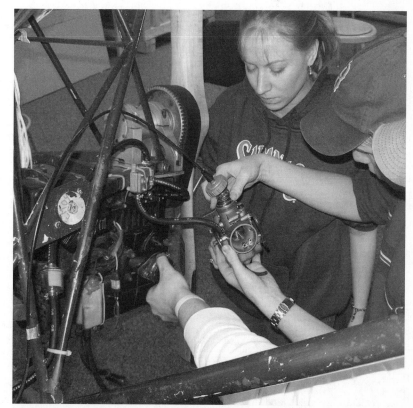

Figure 2-4-1. Those who can perform maintenance on an S-LSA must possess at least a Repairman Certificate with the Maintenance Rating.

FAR	TITLE	DEFINITION
1.1 – 1.2	Definitions and Abbreviations	Provides an understanding of terminology
21.175	Airworthiness certificates: classification	Defines types of airworthiness certificates
21.181	Duration of airworthiness certificates	Limitations of duration of LSA and Experimental certificates
21.190	Issue of a special airworthiness certificate for a light sport category aircraft	This regulation defines what is required of LSA manufacturers to obtain an airworthiness certificate
21.191	Experimental certificates	Defines all types of experimental certificates
21.193	Experimental certificates: general	Defines what must be provided to the FAA when application is made for the ELSA airworthiness certificate
43.1	Applicability of maintenance	Part 43 defines maintenance procedures for LSA
43.3	Persons authorized to perform maintenance	Authorizes certain certificate holders to perform maintenance and preventative maintenance
43.7	Authorized persons to return aircraft to service	LSA repairmen with the maintenance rating may approve an LSA to return to service
43.9	Documentation of maintenance	Defines record entries and record disposition
43.11	Part 91 inspections	Proper endorsement in maintenance records when an inspection is performed
43.13	Maintenance performance	Maintenance should be performed using methods, techniques and practices prescribed in the manufacturer's maintenance manual
43.15	Additional performance rules for inspections	Provides specific guidelines to use when performing part 91 inspections. (Applicable on S-LSA)
43 – App. D	Scope and Detail of items to be included in annual and 100-hour inspections	Broadly describes all items to be inspected in the annual and 100-hour inspections, which are referenced for the condition inspection.
45.11	Identification of aircraft	Identification plate specifications
45.23	Display of marks	Registration number and Experimental or Light Sport markings on aircraft defined
45.27	Display of marks: non fixed-wing aircraft	Powered parachutes and weight shift control aircraft are defined
45.29	Size of marks	Registration marks at least 3" high on ELSA and LSA
65.81	General privileges and limitations of mechanics	Lists the privileges and limitations placed on airframe and powerplant mechanics
65.85	Mechanics: airframe rating	Privileges of mechanics performing maintenance on LSA
65.87	Mechanics: powerplant rating	Privileges of mechanics performing maintenance on LSA
65.107	Repairman certificate: eligibility, privileges, limits	Defines the repairman certificate for light sport aircraft, maintenance and inspection ratings
91.9	Civil aircraft flight manual, marking, placard requirements	Operation of civil aircraft without complying with the manual, markings and placards requirement is prohibited
91.203	Civil aircraft: certifications	Airworthiness certificate requirements – including the display of the certificate in aircraft
91.207	Emergency locator transmitters	Required on fixed-wing S-LSA and ELSA that carry more than one person
91.213	Inoperative instruments	Exemption is granted to certain aircraft regarding the minimum equipment list
91.319	Experimental certificated aircraft: operating limitations	Defines how an experimental aircraft is to be used and inspected
91.327	Special LSA: operating limitations	Defines how a Special – LSA is to be used, inspected and maintained
91.405	Maintenance required	Specifies procedure for handling discrepancies
91.407	Return to service	Proper method for returning an aircraft to service after maintenance
91.417	Maintenance records	Registered aircraft owners must keep several different records related to maintenance

Table 2-5-1. Federal aviation regulations that are applicable to S-LSA and ELSA maintenance and inspections

The consensus standards are referenced directly and indirectly in FAR part 91, by reference to maintenance and operation of the aircraft. For instance, the FARs states that "each person operating an aircraft issued a special airworthiness certificate in the light sport category must operate the aircraft in accordance with the aircraft's operating instructions..." Presumably, the manufacturer will reference the consensus standards in the operating instructions.

Like all experimental aircraft, ELSA are not maintained to an FAA standard, which means there is no formal oversight on the maintenance performed on the aircraft. This is one of the benefits of owning an experimental aircraft: an owner who is competent in maintenance but does not have the time to invest in an FAA approved maintenance course can still work on his/her own airplane and realize additional savings by performing the maintenance themselves. Since LSA aircraft parts are held to an industry-based consensus standard, not the FAA's standard, part costs may be less than a FAA – Parts Manufacturer Approval (PMA) part.

Manufacturers will undoubtedly encourage buyers of ELSA to comply with the consensus standard F2295-03, Continued Operational Safety Monitoring of a Light Sport Airplane, regarding S-LSA maintenance, but this is the owners option.

Section 5
Summary of FAA Regulations

Those who maintain and/or inspect an S-LSA, or inspect an ELSA, should be familiar with the applicable FARs governing their work. Remember, the operating limitations attached to the aircraft airworthiness certificate include other important privileges and limitations as well. Both the FARs and the operating limitations reference the consensus standards, which also provide maintenance and inspection guidance. Federal aviation regulations that are applicable to S-LSA and ELSA maintenance and inspections are presented in Table 2-5-1. The full text of all the FARs can be downloaded from the FAA's website, www.faa.gov.

Chapter 3

AIRFRAME
inspection

Section 1

Airframe Structures

Aircraft have always been designed with weight in mind, and throughout history we have seen novel designs intended to maximize performance and minimize weight. The earliest aircraft such as the Wright Flyers and the Curtiss June Bug had no fuselage, but instead relied on a reinforced central area of the lower wing. Since weight has always been a top priority in aircraft design, the fuselage must be constructed to be as light as possible but still be able to carry flight and landing loads. Wings are subject to bending and flexing, and these loads in turn are carried through to the fuselage at the wing attach points. The inspection of both of these major areas is the focus of this section.

Fuselage Structures

The fuselage of an aircraft is typically defined as the central structure that carries the payload and acts as a basis for mounting the wings, powerplant and tail group. Most aircraft are designed with a single fuselage having a cross-sectional shape that is dictated by the size and weight of the payload. In the case of ultralights, the fuselage may be reduced in cross-sectional area to the dimension of a single box beam or tube, and the payload (pilot and passenger) is located outside of to this structure. A more appropriate term for the supporting structure would be a "keel," similar to the structure in a boat that serves as the basis for the rest of the structure. Figure 3-1-1 (next page) shows the various types of LSA fuselage structures.

Learning Objectives:

- *Airframe Structures*
- *Fuselage Structures*
- *Wing Structures*
- *Inspection Areas*
- *Welded Structures*
- *Composite Structures*
- *Aluminum Structures*
- *Powered Canopies*

Left. Trouble free flights are the result of proper inspection and maintenance.

The three main types of fuselage construction seen in LSA are:

- Welded steel tube
- Composite monocoque
- Aluminum semi-monocoque

Welded steel tube. In this construction method, small-diameter, high-strength steel is welded together in a frame design that provides a load-path capable of carrying the aerodynamic and landing loads, as shown in Figure 3-1-2. The advantage of a steel tube fuselage is that the construction can proceed rapidly with minimal tooling to provide a tailored shape

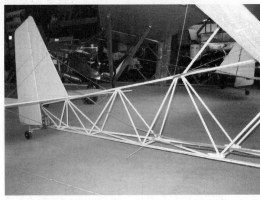

Figure 3-1-2. Small-diameter, high-strength steel frame design

designed for the specific application. As with all truss or frame type structures, the larger the enclosed cross suctional area of the structure, the stiffer the structure becomes and the higher its load carrying capability will be. Welded steel fuselage construction is optimized when the load paths are naturally directed along the primary members of the structure.

To illustrate the advantage of an efficient welded design, Figure 3-1-3 shows two frames, both comprised of 0.625 in. diameter x .065 in. thick welded steel tubing and having outer dimensions of ten inches by three inches. The 200 lb. load is offset from the mounting location on the left-hand side of the frame, requiring the load to be carried through the frame members. In the first figure, the frame is inefficient since the frame loads are directed around the perimeter of the frame. The frame deflects 0.16 in. and has a maximum stress of 67,400 psi. In the second figure, that shows a diagonal member welded across the structure, the same load is carried now with a maximum deflection of 0.017 in. and a stress of 12,700 p.s.i., which is a much safer design for the load.

A structure that is designed with diagonal members must be inspected carefully since the loss of these members would result in an overstress condition and possible failure. It is therefore important in the inspection to ensure that all members of a welded frame structure are intact and carrying their intended design loads. The lesson can be applied to all structures, where the original design with its intended load paths optimized for strength should always be observed.

Composite monocoque. A monocoque fuselage structure represents the most advanced of fuselage designs, with all loads from the wings and tail group being distributed through the structure's load-bearing skin.

Composite technology has made monocoque construction more common since the materials can be tailored to carry the loads through

(A)

(B)

(C)

Figure 3-1-1. Various types of LSA fuselage structures: (A) Welded steel tube (B) Composite monocoque (C) Aluminum semimonocoque

Photo B courtesy of Flight Star USA

the outer shell of the fuselage. Other aircraft construction materials prefer straight lines and simple angles in their design, which limits the ability to conduct loads through the outer form of the aircraft. Composite sailplanes have been constructed using monocoque technology, and the Beechcraft Starship, designed by Scaled Composites, LLC which first flew in 1986, represented the first large-scale passenger aircraft to be constructed as a monocoque design. Figure 3-1-4 shows a composite carbon monocoque fuselage from a current LSA in production.

Construction techniques using external molds (tooling) to control the surface finish of a composite structure have now become commonplace for the highest performance aircraft. Figure 3-1-5 shows a typical the manufacturing process for a light-sport aircraft, where an entire half fuselage is produced by laying down layers of woven cloth and epoxy to cure in a mold.

While the composite monocoque construction is ideally suited to LSA from a strength to weight aspect, it has some drawbacks from the inspection and repair standpoints. With all the loads being carried by the structure of the skin, prompt

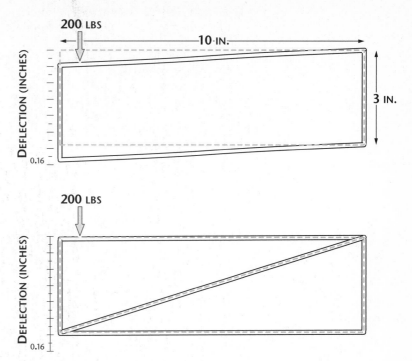

Figure 3-1-3. Load distribution of welded steel tube structure

attention to restoring the original design characteristics during a repair is very important.

Aluminum semi-monocoque. More commonly associated with the Cessna and Piper-type aircraft, a common aluminum airframe construction technique involves building a frame of stringers and bulkheads which are then skinned with a thin sheet of aluminum. Figure 3-1-6 shows the skeleton of an aluminum semi-monocoque airframe that provides stiffness and strength in the outer shell of the

Figure 3-1-4. Monocoque fuselage constructed from carbon fiber.

Figure 3-1-5. Manufacturing process used to create a modern composite structure.

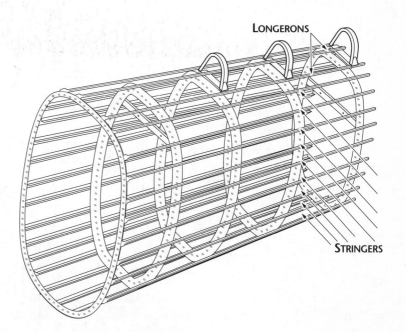

Figure 3-1-6. Skeleton of an aluminum semi-monocoque airframe.

fuselage while keeping weight to a minimum. The most common method of assembling a structure such as this is through riveting, although structural adhesives have also been used effectively and friction stir welding has recently been employed to bond stringers to aircraft skin. Figure 3-1-7 shows the inside of a semi-monocoque fuselage revealing its light-weight, high strength design. While the semi-monocoque structure has some disadvantages from a construction aspect, (more parts and labor), there are also significant advantages.

Since the loads are shared by multiple parts of the structure, a single point failure usually does not result in catastrophic consequences. The use of accepted and known repair techniques for sheet metal and rivets is an attractive benefit as well.

On many aircraft, similarities exist in the construction of an aircraft fuselage and the wings because they both attempt to carry a maximum load with minimal weight. Wings are predominantly either cantilever beam struc-

Figure 3-1-7. Lightweight, high strength design of a semi-monocoque fuselage.

Figure 3-1-8. Typical wood wing construction

tures or externally braced structures that carry mainly transverse loads through a slender spar arrangement. One notable exception to this design is for powered parachutes, where the wing gains strength in the tension created by an inflated flexible structure. LSA encompasses just about every wing type in existence.

Wing Structures

The structures that are covered in the LSA wing inspection include the following:

- Wood structures
- Fabric coverings
- Aluminum structures
- Composite structures
- Powered parachute canopies

Wood structures. Wood and fabric was a popular construction method in the early days of aviation because of its lightweight strength and availability. The same applies today, with wood having a higher strength-to-weight ratio than aluminum when bending stress is considered. For this reason wood is still used for aerobatic aircraft. Figure 3-1-8 shows typical wood wing construction. The downside of wood wing construction is the environmental degradation, making it almost mandatory to hangar these aircraft.

Fabric coverings. Fabric covered wings have been in existence since the earliest days of aviation, when Otto Lilienthal used a tightly woven fabric on the bamboo and wood airframes he constructed for hang gliding experiments in the 1890s. The Wright brothers continued in this tradition, and aircraft today are commonly designed with fabric coverings to reduce weight while providing an airtight seal over the airframe.

Fabric covering may come in several different forms, with "Grade A" cotton fabric being the standard recognized by the FAA in most traditional aircraft applications. Grade A fabric is a 4 oz. mercerized fabric made of high-grade, long staple cotton. It contains 80 to 84 threads per in. and has a minimum tensile strength of 80 lb./in. of width. The use of cotton fabric combined with "dopes" to shrink the material for a tight fit on the wing has been part of aircraft construction since the 1920s. Today, modern materials are used to cover aircraft including Dacron and Polyester fabrics, which are stronger and less susceptible to rotting deterioration than Grade A cotton.

Aluminum structures. In the inspection of aluminum wings, three categories exist: the

Figure 3-1-9. Built-up wing section.

Figure 3-1-10. Fabric covered, aluminum tube construction

built-up wing design, tube spar design and the braced tube and fabric structure.

Built-up wing section

The built-up wing consists of an internal beam member, or spar, that is designed to carry the bending and shear loads, while the aluminum skin carries torsional loads. The wing shape is maintained with ribs. Figure 3-1-9 shows an example of this. Aluminum wings that are fabric covered usually have a forward and aft spar, and strut bracing so that the torsional loads can be supported without relying on the skin, as shown in Figure 3-1-10.

Figure 3-1-11. Tube spar wing construction

Figure 3-1-12. Typical tube spar ultralight

Figure 3-1-13. An LSA candidate with wire braced tube spar wing.

Tube spar design

The tube spar design has found a niche in certain aircraft types, including homebuilts, ultralights, and a limited set of production aircraft. The Bede series of propeller-driven aircraft, designed by Jim Bede and manufactured by a variety of companies were certificated, production aircraft incorporating an aluminum tube spar with aluminum skins that were bonded to the ribs, which in turn were bonded to the spar. See Figure 3-1-11. The most common usage of the tube spar design has been in the ultralight community, due to its low cost, availability and simplified construction technique. A typical tube spar ultralight is shown in Figure 3-1-12.

Wings of these two types, built up and tubular spar, can be optimized for loads and aerodynamics, but at a cost. More complex geometry requires more expensive tooling, and so many aluminum wing structures have a basic, simple geometry. The advantages of composites over aluminum are most important in the manufacturing process. A complex geometry in a composite mold may only be slightly more difficult to produce than a simple geometry, giving the designer added freedom in design optimization. The load carrying abilities of the composite structure exceeds the aluminum structure, with a significant weight savings.

Braced tube and fabric. Weight shift aircraft, or trikes, commonly have a tube spar that is strut or wire braced to provide adequate stiffness and strength. These designs are similar to many ultralights in that they have a Dacron wing, but this wing is flexible and will be stiffened with battens instead of permanently mounted ribs. These aircraft are very similar to hang gliders, with a foldable wing that can be reduced to a small package for easy transportation. Figure 3-1-13 shows the typical double surfaced design, with batten-stiffening and wire bracing. The wing frame consists of leading edge tube spars and a cross-bar, visible as a shadow within the wing.

Composite structures. Composite construction technology is ideally suited to wings where shapes can be optimized and smooth surface finishes maintain the laminar flow over the wing. Unlike other types of wing construction that can flex and bend, changing the shape of the airfoil and how it reacts with the air, the composite wing remains very stiff. As a wing flexes in response to aerodynamic forces, its shape can change and result in higher drag which degrades the aircraft's performance. The wing that uses composite materials and construction has a built in rigidity that resists the forces trying to deform it. The result is an airfoil that is designed for optimum lift and speed without having to be over engineered to compensate for the negative effects created by aerodynamics. Composite wings are similar to aluminum structures in that they frequently have a main spar, which carries the majority of the bending loads, and thinner wing skins, which carry torsional loads. Figure 3-1-14 shows the inside of a composite wing with the main spar exposed, and composite ribs similar to what is found in an aluminum wing molded into the structure. Composite wings have some of the same inspection requirements of a composite fuselage.

Powered parachute canopies. Powered parachutes were introduced in the 1980s and have become a popular option for sport pilots because of their simplicity. This simplicity allows an operator to drive to the airfield with the trike in tow, remove the trike from a trailer, unfold the canopy, and be in the air 15 minutes after arriving at the field. Operators of powered parachutes are quick to point out this low impact nature as a major draw to the sport.

The inspection of the canopy and associated hardware found on a powered parachute has several common connections to the sky diving community as well as to powered aircraft, making the inspections unique.

Section 2

Inspection Areas

The need for periodic, in-depth, inspections of any aircraft has long been established as necessary for safe, enjoyable flight. Anyone who has found a critical part that is worn or broken will attest to this concept.

An inspection program that is based on flight hours or calendar intervals has one overriding rule – it must be conducted as stipulated. There can be no short cuts or temporary fixes, since one of the basic objectives is to return the aircraft to its design standards.

The tools required for any inspection begin with the knowledge and understanding of the aircraft and how it is built, as well as experience. A comprehensive checklist is fundamental for any inspection since the reliance on memory is not enough. A checklist is a written record of what has been looked at and what has not. Just as important is a record of what defects or problems were found and how they were corrected. This also makes the logbook recording easier to write. An in-depth review of the aircraft records or past maintenance corrections or alterations should also precede any inspection. By reviewing the records, areas that have been a source of concern can be pinpointed for special attention. Alterations can be looked at

to make sure they are not creating problems with the rest of the aircraft.

Some of the other tools that should be assembled for an inspection include a good extendable, flexible, mirror and a bright flashlight. These are the two most used tools during any inspection. A magnifying glass with at least a ten-power magnification can help in determining if a suspect crack is a crack or just a scratch. Additionally, a blunt probe, a borescope, composite tap test tool and a fabric tester are other items that may contribute to a more successful inspection.

Inspection of Welded Steel Tube Structures

Any tubular steel structure that has been welded needs to be inspected carefully for problems relating to corrosion, cracks and overloading of the structure.

Corrosion. Steel members are most susceptible to general surface corrosion, or rust, where paint has been removed and bare metal has been exposed, as shown in Figure 3-2-1. The loss of paint and primer, in small, localized areas can have the effect of creating a stress concentration as material thickness is reduced through corrosion. Scratches in steel structures should be examined carefully, using a magnifying glass, to verify that deeper corrosion has not occurred. High-strength steel parts that have been heat treated for certain strength

Figure 3-1-14. Composite wing structure

Figure 3-2-1. Corrosion due to exposed bare metal

Figure 3-2-2. Galvanic corrosion on a bottom frame tube

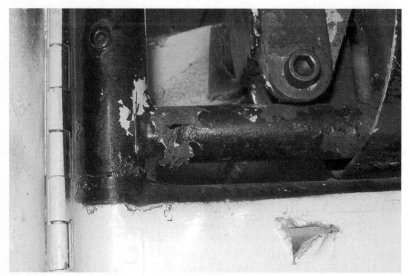

Figure 3-2-3. Perforation at a welded joint

JURY STRUTS

Figure 3-2-4. Jury struts increase the buckling strength of a member

in areas exposed to water or dampness, such as the bottom frame tube of the ultralight shown in Figure 3-2-2.

On many aircraft, the tubular structure may have been drilled where bolts or fittings are attached. These holes allow moisture to enter the tubing and internal corrosion to begin. Internal corrosion is very difficult to inspect for and is often only found when the structure fails. The best cure in these cases is through prevention. All holes must be sealed to help prevent moisture from entering the tubes. Over time even the daily temperature and humidity changes can create enough condensation inside the tubes to have active corrosion.

Wing strut brackets at the base of a tubular wing strut frequently form a cap which will prevent the drainage of any moisture from inside the strut. In the case of a bracket that is welded to the base of the strut, the potential for rusting and perforation is significant. Past airworthiness directives on vintage Piper aircraft have addressed this very problem, where aging airframes tied down outside have experienced significant corrosion around the lower end of the strut. In an inspection of a steel wing strut, the tubes should be smooth and have no evidence of paint bubbling or blistering. Applying pressure to questionable areas should not show any evidence of yielding or break-through.

At welded joints, concentration cell corrosion (crevice corrosion) can take place caused by the contact of the tube and the weld materials. Welds tend to be more susceptible to corrosion due to many factors, including the relative size of the weld material to the parent material, so careful attention should be placed on inspecting welds.

Welds, by their nature, are a disruption in the normal metallurgy of the area. The area around the weld, and the weld itself, has been heated and then fused together with the addition of a filler material. This creates a local stress concentration that can be a source of not only corrosion but also cracks. More often than not, cracks appear at the edge of the welds, so that area should be inspected very carefully with a magnifying glass and a strong light.

Again, when welded joints are exposed to moisture the rate of corrosion will increase, and these areas need special attention. Figure 3-2-3 shows complete perforation at a welded joint on an ultralight frame.

The removal of surface rust in those areas that can be treated using the manufacturer's recommendations can significantly reduce any stress concentrations. The aircraft-specific guidelines must be followed in all cases. Obviously, there are limits to salvaging corroded metal, and these limits should be observed.

properties will suffer the most from rusted surface scratches. These parts gain an added measure of strength because of the surface finish, so any corrosion of pitting can affect these components.

In cases where water has been allowed to penetrate the painted steel surface, galvanic corrosion can be detected by bubbling or blistering of the paint where oxides have formed. Close inspection should be performed on tubes that have water marks on them, or are known to be

Overstress. Aircraft subjected to loads that exceed what they were designed for may show signs of an overstressed condition, resulting in a yielding of the material. Steel tube structures that have been overstressed may indicate evidence of this loading condition through wrinkled paint and, of course, a bend or bow in an otherwise straight tube. The seriousness of this type of damage cannot be overemphasized: a tube that is bent will have a dramatically reduced strength in compression, resulting in a greatly weakened structure. This is called column buckling and is always a concern for long, slender members in compression, but is more serious if the member has an initial bend that can graduate into buckling.

Buckling can be demonstrated with a coffee stir stick. It is probably impossible to pull on a plastic stir stick and cause it to break, but squeeze it between your fingers and it collapses immediately. The same is true for tubes and struts in aircraft structures.

Buckling strength is increased by reducing the length of the column. If the column length is reduced by one-half, the strength in compression is increased by a factor of four. Wing struts on aircraft frequently have smaller struts attached in the middle called jury struts to increase the buckling strength of the member as shown in Figure 3-2-4. By effectively pinning the strut in the middle, the wing can now safely support negative "g" loads.

Because buckling happens when the member distorts laterally, any tube that has a bend or dent will potentially fail sooner because the failure mechanism is already initiated. Tube structures that experience compressive loading should be carefully inspected for defects that can accelerate a buckling failure.

Tubes can be bent from hard landing damage, foreign object debris on takeoff and landing roll, pilot ingress/egress damage, and damage from in-flight loads and bird strikes. Examination of tube structures with these loading scenarios in mind will aid in the inspection of the airframe. Any tube that is bent from non-design loads must be repaired or replaced prior to passing the LSA inspection.

Dented tubes can result from rocks that are thrown up in the take-off and landing rolls, and even when a mechanic drops a wrench a dent in a structural tube could result. Other localized damage can occur if there is reduced clearance between a tube and another part that come into contact through vibration, causing wear and reduced wall thickness on the weaker of the two members. Engine exhaust components should be checked to ensure that they will not contact members such as the engine mount in extreme vibration events such as engine start-up.

Inspection of Fittings

Highly stressed components are common on aircraft, where loads must be efficiently transferred from member to member. Bolted joints frequently transfer loads from lightweight frame members to concentrated weights, such as the engine. These joints represent areas that must be thoroughly inspected because they are critical to safe operation.

Bolts should not show any wear that would indicate they are getting smaller in diameter and consequently getting weaker. This type of wear is common if the bolted material is harder than the bolt, but it will also exist at a lower level if the bolted material is softer also. Nuts should be installed with the recommended torque and the correct locking feature to ensure they do not loosen. Nylon locknuts have an undersized plastic collar that keeps them from backing off, and high temperature locknuts have a deformed or serrated cap on the nut that acts to jam the threads. Make sure you are using the right kind of nut for the application, since nylon locknuts will not last long when exposed to high temperatures.

Castellated nuts have slots so that a cotter key can be inserted through the bolt to lock the nut onto the bolt. These are most common when the nut is not torqued, such as with landing gear scissors links or pinned joints. Figure 3-2-5 shows a castellated nut and three locknuts on a wing spar attachment. Note that at between 1 and 3 threads extend beyond the end of the nut. This is standard practice and should be part of all inspections to ensure a bolt is firmly engaged in the nut locking feature.

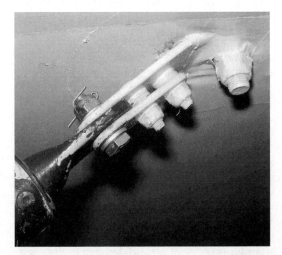

Figure 3-2-5. Castellated nut and three locknuts on a wing spar attachment

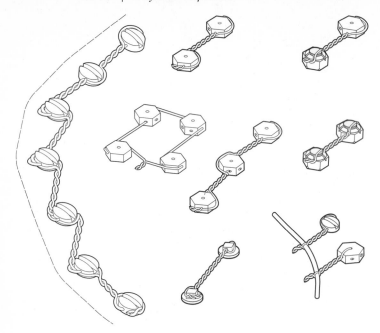

Figure 3-2-6. Safety wiring patterns

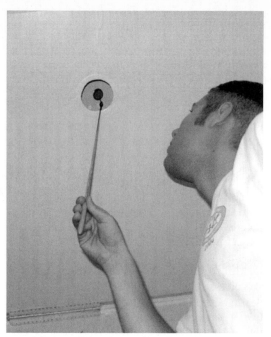

Figure 3-2-8. Telescoping inspection mirror

If the bolt needs to be locked in place, it will have a drilled head and safety wire must be used to prevent it from backing out. These are common on propeller installations and on the engine, both of which have high vibration levels that can loosen fasteners. Use the correct sized safety wire for the application, with some guidance coming from the FAA's Advisory Circular AC 43.13-1b, Acceptable Methods, Techniques, and Practices, Aircraft Inspection and Repair. Figure 3-2-6 shows samples of acceptable safety wiring patterns, which should consist of a wire twist of 6 to 8 turns per inch. This AC also contains information on identifying bolts to determine if the correct type of bolt has been installed.

Rod end bearings are commonly found on aircraft, not only on control systems as will be discussed in a future section, but also as a means of coupling structural members. The concept of the rod end bearing is to allow a degree of freedom to account for flexibility while still transmitting high forces. Figure 3-2-7 shows a rod end bearing that is part of a landing gear system which has developed a small crack. Inspecting fittings such as this may require

magnification, since small cracks can develop close to the bearing surface, making detection difficult. Again, always carefully inspect areas where connections are made since these are highly stressed areas.

Inspection of Composite Structures

Many composite structures are difficult to inspect, since the two halves of an aerodynamically shaped component are typically molded first and then bonded together in a tight, efficient form. The resulting structure has enclosed cavities with little or no provision for inspection, so the inspector must rely on clues provided by the exterior of the part. A telescoping inspection mirror, Figure 3-2-8, is an extremely valuable tool to visually inspect interior parts that are impossible to see in a direct visual path. In some cases, a fiber optic borescope may be needed to see into tight spaces. Inspections should concentrate on discontinuities in the structure, where fittings are molded into the structure and where reinforced joints occur.

Often the internal problems are manifested by certain surface irregularities like cracks, blisters and wrinkles. A good understanding of surface defects and inspection procedures is necessary when looking at composite structures.

Surface damage. A visual inspection of composite structure surfaces frequently will verify whether there is structural damage requiring a repair. An effective technique of detecting damage is to illuminate the surface in question with a strong light source aimed at an angle to the

Figure 3-2-7. Rod end bearing with a small crack

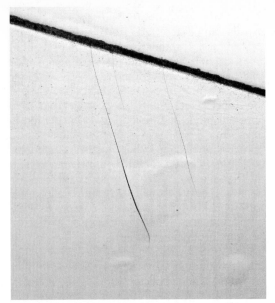

Figure 3-2-9. Bubbling in a composite surface and the resulting cracks

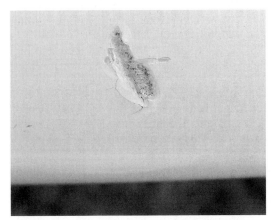

Figure 3-2-10. Leading edge impact damage

surface. When the surface is viewed from a few feet away, surface defects will become apparent in the reflection and shadowing of the beam. Depth variations of 0.012″ have been shown to be reliably detected using this technique especially when the surface is illuminated from several different locations. This technique cannot always detect interior damage, and so all exposed composite surfaces (inside and outside the aircraft) should be inspected to increase the likelihood of finding a structural defect. Delaminations resulting in a bubbling of the surface can be detected in this manner. Figure 3-2-9 shows a composite surface that has evidence of bubbling and an initiated crack.

Figure 3-2-10 shows leading edge impact damage which has removed a small piece of the finish coat on the wing of this airplane. To avoid stress concentrations and damage that may propagate deeper into the wing structure, this divot should be treated as recommended by the manufacturer. At this point, the structural repair manual, or SRM, should be mentioned.

18.1 Structural Repair
18.2 Repair Criteria

Although this section outlines repair permissible on structure of the aircraft, the decision of whether to repair or replace a major unit of structure will be influenced by such factors as time and labor available, and by a comparison of labor costs with the price of replacement assemblies. Past experience indicates that replacement, in many cases, is less costly than major repair. Certainly, when the aircraft must be restored to its airworthy condition in a limited length of time, replacement is preferable. Restoration of a damaged aircraft to its original design strength, shape, and alignment involves careful evaluation of the damage, followed by exacting workmanship in performing the repairs. This section suggests the extent of structural repair practicable on the aircraft, and supplements Federal Aviation Regulation, Part 43. Consult the factory when in doubt about a repair not specifically mentioned here.

18.3 General Consideration for Composite Repair

All major and structural components of the aircraft are carbon-fiber or glass-fiber construction. We strongly recommend the replacement of components when structural damage is detected or return to factory for repair. Repair to non-structural components may be accomplished using factory specified materials. Observe the resin manufacturer's recommendations concerning mixing and application of the resin. Epoxy resin is mandatory for making repairs, since epoxy compounds are usually more stable and predictable than polyester and, in addition, give better adhesion.

18.4 Equipment and Tools

18.5 Support Stands

Padded, reinforced sawhorse or tripod type support stands, sturdy enough to support any assembly placed upon them, must be used to store a removed wing or stabilizer. The fuselage, must NOT be supported from the underside, since the skin is not designed for this purpose. Adapt support stands to fasten to the wing-attach points or landing gear attach-points when supporting a fuselage.

Figure 3-2-11. Excerpt from a composite aircraft manufacturer's manual

The manufacturers of composite aircraft will typically publish an SRM or other guidelines that allow a determination to be made on the severity of the composite damage, and what, if any, repairs are required. Damage to certain parts of a composite airframe may be deemed acceptable since they exist in low-stress areas, non-critical for flight safety. For instance, abrasion on the bottom of the fuselage of a glider caused by "nosing" it over on the landing roll-out for speed control often amounts to acceptable wear. Critical and non-critical areas for maintenance should be spelled out by the manufacturer to assist the owner in determining whether damage is negligible, repairable, or non-repairable. Figure 3-2-11 shows sample guidelines published in a composite aircraft manufacturer's repair manual.

Figure 3-2-12. Bushing molded into a composite wing shows evidence of disbond.

Figure 3-2-13. Example of disbond

Surface defects may also occur due to erosion, where parts are in close contact with each other resulting in frictional wear. Cowling and fairing attach points should be carefully inspected as these are places where sliding friction may occur if proper isolation such as "chafe tape" does not exist. Erosion may also be found on the leading edges of the airframe, where rain and frozen precipitation can wear away the outer surface of a composite during flight. These conditions frequently lead to other types of degradation, such as delamination when water seeps into an exposed composite fiber matte and freezes at altitude. The presence of erosion should be noted and corrective actions immediately taken to prevent further wear, as it can lead to more extensive damage and a higher cost repair as it progresses.

Disbonds. In addition to surface defects, disbonds can be detected effectively using visual techniques. The most serious type of disbond is found in the separation of a composite material from a dissimilar material, such as honeycomb, aluminum or steel. Disbonds may also occur between the finish coat, or gel coat of the airplane, and the first load-carrying composite layer. In the case where metallic elements are molded into a composite structure, evidence of a disbond can be found by applying pressure to the element and observing if there is any relative motion. Figure 3-2-12 shows a load-carrying bushing molded into a composite wing; with evidence of free play provided by the loss of paint around the bushing. This is a particularly serious condition, since bushings such as this presumably carry major loads within the airframe. The inspector should be careful to examine these areas perhaps with magnification for any evidence of looseness.

Figure 3-2-13 shows a dramatic disbond occurring between the finish gel coat and the first structural composite layer of a home-built aircraft. In this case, the finish coat is so thick that in a vibration environment it created high separation forces with the fiberglass layer. There may have been improper conditioning of the bond surface as well, which would have reduced the strength of the bond between the gel coat and the fiberglass layer. Yet another example of a disbond of this type is shown in Figure 3-2-14.

Delamination. Delamination damage may be detected visually, but a better technique to find internal damage is the tap test, which involves tapping the composite surface with a coin or thick washer at least one inch in diameter and 0.1" thick. Some after market retailers carry a small "tap test" hammer for composites that can be used as well. Tapping at intervals

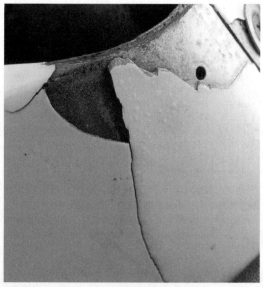

Figure 3-2-14. Disbond of the gel coat

of approximately ¼" will reveal damage by a change in the sound of the material as it is struck. Areas of a good bond will sound clear and have a high frequency "ring". Those areas that have a bonding discrepancy will sound dull and have a lower frequency sound. The method works well on skins that are bonded to honeycomb, and in detecting delamination a few layers below the surface. It seems to be a reliable indication of heat damage as well, mainly because damage of this type penetrates the first few layers of material from the surface. Thicker composite parts with delamination occurring more than a few layers below the surface will be difficult to detect using the tap method. Figure 3-2-15 shows the proper tap technique.

An example of delamination is shown in Figure 3-2-16, presumably where a bracket that was embedded in the composite material pulled the fiberglass layers apart under load. The suspicion in this case is that the bonding surface was not properly treated before the final glass laminate was applied.

Crazing. Crazing is characterized by surface cracking due to brittle resins that have an elongation less than the fiber type used in the composite. Since strain is highest at its surface, any flexing of a composite structure may cause the surface to develop small cracks if a relatively stiff resin has been used in the finish. Ultraviolet exposure can enhance the brittleness of resins, leading to the small, regular surface cracks shown in Figure 3-2-17.

Crazing at best will lead to slightly increased aerodynamic drag, but at worst can precipitate failure of the matrix below the cracked surface. Stress concentrations may be created which affect the composite, leading to a potential failure of the underlying plies as shown in Figure

Figure 3-2-15 Tap testing to detect delamination

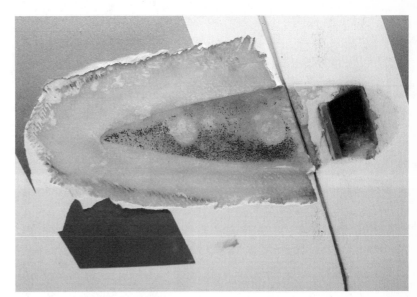

Figure 3-2-16. Delamination

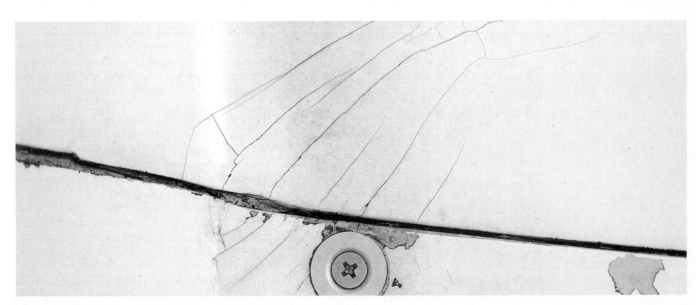

Figure 3-2-17. Surface cracks likely caused by ultraviolet exposure.

Figure 3-2-18. An example of a stress concentration crack in a landing gear fairing.

Figure 3-2-19. Inadequate epoxy in lay-up

Figure 3-2-20. Significant delamination

3-2-18. This figure also shows that flexible structures (fairings, for example) are more susceptible to hairline cracks leading to serious structural damage as opposed to structures that are thicker and stiffer. Thin composite structures showing evidence of crazing should be monitored, and a refinishing job may be necessary to halt the crack propagation.

Heat damage. Composite structures may experience significant strength degradation when exposed to temperatures above the upper service temperature, typically around 350°F. When a composite structure is exposed to temperature this high, it may not appear to be damaged from a visual inspection, but its strength properties have been greatly reduced nonetheless. At higher temperatures, such as those caused by a lightning strike, resin may be completely vaporized, leaving only bare fabric which cannot carry any compressive loads at all. Moisture is found in all composites, and this can cause additional interlaminar stress when the moisture is vaporized at high heat levels, leading to delamination.

It may be easy to find high temperature exposure in a composite where the evidence is unmistakable: a lightning strike or charred material would indicate severe heat damage. But long-term high temperature exposure that does not lead to an obvious surface blemish may be nearly impossible to detect without sophisticated test equipment, even though strength may be seriously degraded. Inspection of composite airframes should always anticipate the possibility of a high temperature situation, such as a leaking exhaust system, so that if a problem exists there would be a better chance of detecting it.

Moisture ingress. Moisture tends to reduce the stiffness of a composite material, and also its strength. As a result, care should be taken in examining composite structures that have been exposed to water or moisture for prolonged periods. Composites will have a tendency to absorb water if microscopic defects in the structure exist, such as pin holes caused by an inadequate amount of epoxy used in the lay-up process. Figure 3-2-19 shows a control surface that not only has evidence of pin holes, but is also beginning to delaminate on the right side.

Trailing edges of control surfaces are another area requiring careful examination, since a small opening caused by delamination can result in significant water absorption and a possible adverse balance situation that may lead to control surface flutter. Figure 3-2-20 shows significant delamination on an exposed composite edge, a defect accelerated by the presence of moisture.

The use of composite materials for aircraft has a relatively short history, compared to aluminum.

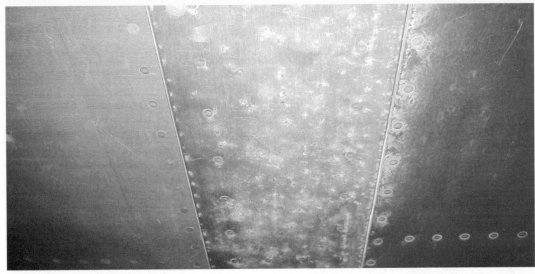

Figure 3-2-21. Surface corrosion

There is still much to be learned about inspection and repair techniques in this young field.

Inspection of Aluminum Structures

Aluminum has been used in aircraft for decades and a tremendous amount of research has been done in the areas of corrosion control, failure modes and inspections. There are three areas that deserve added attention: corrosion control, the effect of fatigue on aluminum and the consequences of overstressing an aluminum structure. Since aluminum is rarely used in an unalloyed state, corrosion is the most important of these three areas.

Corrosion. Surface corrosion is just as common on aluminum structures as it is on steel structures, where the oxide is a white, powdery residue instead of red rust. Aluminum structures that are not primed, painted or anodized will be subject to this type of corrosion and may show significant degradation if the surface is repeatedly exposed to moisture. A common mechanism of surface corrosion is found in the hangar, where condensation forms on a cold aircraft wing even though the airplane is indoors. The Blanik sailplane is notorious for developing significant corrosion on the underside of its wings, even though most sailplane owners keep their aircraft in a hangar. Figure 3-2-21 shows an example of this type of corrosion.

Surface corrosion usually progresses slowly and has a minimal impact on the integrity of the structure if it appears only on the aluminum surface, but once detected it should be treated to avoid further degradation such as pitting. Pitting is a localized corrosion phenomenon that may extend deep into a structure, seriously affecting the structure's strength properties. A review of the information on types of corrosion shows that almost all failures related to corrosion begin with the presence of surface pitting. The pits represent a breach in the surface that allows the entry of moisture and acids to the rest of the metal. Preserving the integrity of the surface is key to preventing further problems. A magnified cross-section is shown in Figure 3-2-22.

Riveted joints can be the source of several types of corrosion, requiring careful inspection for signs of damage. Aluminum rivets are most commonly used on aircraft structures, although around highly stressed areas such as the wing carry-through structure or firewall, steel alloy rivets may also be used. When aluminum rivets are in contact with the aluminum

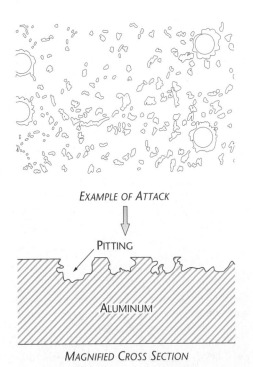

EXAMPLE OF ATTACK

PITTING

ALUMINUM

MAGNIFIED CROSS SECTION

Figure 3-2-22. Pitting

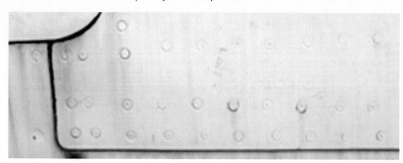

Figure 3-2-23. Oxide residue emanating from a riveted joint; known as smoking rivets

Figure 3-2-24. Filiform corrosion

aircraft structure and there is slight movement between the surfaces, frictional wear and corrosive action can occur and seriously degrade the strength of the riveted joint.

Corrosion around rivets in a wing may see the most severe environment of any riveted joint because of water damage and flexing. The wing on an aircraft is designed to be stiff, but that is a relative term. The fuselage may be an order of magnitude (10x) stiffer, and the possibility of relative motion in rivet joints will be much greater in the wing than in the fuselage. A close inspection should be conducted of the riveted joints along the wing spar where stresses are known to be high and fretting corrosion may take place.

Fretting corrosion is the result of slight movement of aluminum on aluminum (or other similar metals) where an oxide is formed that acts as an abrasive material to further degrade the integrity of the riveted joint. The oxide resulting from aluminum fretting corrosion is black, and it is easy to detect because a black residue will appear around the head of the rivet. This is an excellent indicator that there may be a loose rivet and corrective action needs to be taken. Figure 3-2-23 shows evidence of an oxide residue emanating from a riveted joint. This is also known as "smoking rivets" and should be corrected.

Usually rivets are chosen to minimize the likelihood of galvanic corrosion between the rivet and the riveted material, but in moist environments and coastal locations, galvanic corrosion may appear around a riveted joint. This may start as a small crack observed in the paint around a rivet head, but further degradation results in a bubbling of the paint around the rivet head.

Filiform corrosion is a form of an oxygen concentration cell that shows a worm-like trace of corrosion products below an organic finish, such as polyurethane paint. This corrosion can develop deeper into the material and take the form of intergranular corrosion, which is corrosion identified at the grain boundaries of a metal on a microscopic scale. High humidity environments (greater than 70%) aid in the corrosion process, and high strength aluminum alloys such as 2014 and 7075 are more susceptible to intergranular corrosion, requiring more attention during the inspection. Figure 3-2-24 shows this type of corrosion. Intergranular corrosion is one of the more insidious forms of corrosion since it can travel along the grain boundaries and remain undetected until it is evidenced by exfoliation. Aluminum casting and extrusions that are subject to high stress loads are more susceptible to intergranular corrosion than other forms of aluminum.

Exfoliation is an advanced form of intergranular corrosion that results in the metal developing distinct layers as corrosion products expand and cause the metal to lose its integrity. It is easily detected by the apparent formation of layers of material aligned in a direction of the rolling or extrusion process, typical of most aircraft parts. Figure 3-2-25 shows an example of exfoliation. Often this means the replacement of a part as opposed to a repair.

The assessment of corrosion damage can be a complex process if specific details on how to assess damage are not provided by the manufacturer. On the fuselage, aluminum skin carries loads over a large surface and so the stress levels tend to be low. Allowable corrosion limits are higher on the skin for this reason as opposed to a higher stressed member such as stringers, bulkheads, or the wing carry-through structure. On these parts, any corrosion may be determined to be unacceptable due the critical nature of their load carrying capability.

Typical areas where the fuselage is more susceptible to corrosion include:

- The exhaust trail (downstream of the engine exhaust). The by products of combustion, carbon, lead salts and bromides create a chemical soup that when mixed with moisture will corrode aluminum in a very short time.

- The battery compartment vent area. Sulfuric acid, both liquid and vapor, is one of the worst chemicals to put into contact with aluminum. Keeping this area clean and neutralized is a simple, necessary preventative action.

- Areas where water may accumulate, such as the belly of the fuselage. The belly, or bilge area of an aircraft will have dirt lying in it. This dirt traps moisture against the skin, which results in surface corrosion.

- Near the landing gear where the tires may pick up debris and lodge it in the airframe

These areas are prone to damage of the protective paint, which then exposes the bare aluminum. Dirt and debris lodged in these areas trap moisture against the skin.

Finding corrosion in a wing is more challenging than for the fuselage due to the small size and inaccessibility of parts of the wing interior. The use of mirrors as mentioned and possibly a borescope will become necessary to check fittings inside of the wing and other areas susceptible to corrosion. One "trick" commonly employed in a wing inspection is to tap the bottom of the wing with your hand and listen for any debris that may be dislodged and set in motion by the flexing of the wing skin. Any time there is evidence of animals such as birds or rodents in the airframe, the area should be very carefully examined for localized corrosion. Waste products from animals are not kind to metal structures, accelerating the rate at which corrosion will occur. The debris could be a bird's nest, a hornet's nest, a mouse nest, or even some other life form that has taken up residence in the aircraft. Worse yet, the loose item may be a part of the wing structure itself or a tool that was left inside the wing during construction. A more thorough inspection would follow if debris was found in this manner. Likewise, if dirt has accumulated in the wing it should be removed and close examination of the area should be made.

The assessment of corrosion damage on the wing is no easier than it was on the fuselage. Again, the first source of information regarding how much corrosion is acceptable should be obtained from the manufacturer. Typical areas on the wing susceptible to corrosion include:

- The root (fuselage-end) where water may collect due to the dihedral angle of the wing. This area often is not ventilated well because of the way it is constructed.

- Near the landing gear where the tires can pick up debris and lodge it in the airframe

- Enclosed areas of the wing that can trap moisture and sustain a relatively high humidity level. Closed bays in a wing should have a drain hole that serves to ventilate the wing as well as drain any water.

- The underside of the wing where condensation often forms leading to galvanic corrosion. The underside of the top skin also is a prime area for condensation, particularly under any dark paint schemes since these areas cool rapidly.

Fatigue. Fatigue is a failure mechanism caused by repeated, cyclic loading of a part where any single cycle does not exceed the static strength of the part. It is the repeated application of low-stress inputs that eventually causes a part to fail suddenly, similar to a brittle material failure. Because of the lack of warning in a fatigue failure, the aerospace industry takes them seriously. The most dangerous fatigue situation is when a main load carrying element fails, such as the wing spar. Since aluminum technically does not have an "endurance limit," all aluminum parts will eventually fail under cyclic loading regardless of the magnitude of the load input. Why, then, do we fly aluminum aircraft? Because they are designed with a factor of safety which guarantees they will last much longer than normal operation permits. In some cases, such as with aging fire bombers and World War II aircraft, fatigue failures have claimed lives because of the severe environment these aircraft have operated under their entire lives. However, with the same type of aircraft that are flown within their original design specifications, these dramatic failures rarely occur.

More common fatigue failures occur on non-critical airframe components, such as where a sudden transition from a stiff support to a weak support will cause a concentrated stress around the transition area. On the fuselage, this would happen where a riveted sheet metal skin has significant stiffness and support around the bulkhead, but little stiffness or support away from the bulkhead. Flexing of the unsupported skin will lead to high stresses developing around the rivets where the skin is held rigid, and this may cause fatigue cracking in the aluminum. Rivet lines may form lengthy stress concentrations that could result in catastrophic airframe failure, which is what happened on an Aloha Airlines 737 in 1988. It is important to inspect for the potential of a crack line forming where a

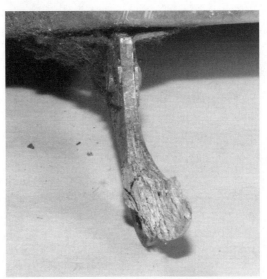

Figure 3-2-25. Severe exfoliation has rendered this part unusable.

row of rivets or fasteners exists by examining for a small-radius bend or paint crack in the sheet metal aligned with the fastener line.

Similar to the fuselage inspection, it is important to examine areas where flexing is present on the wing which can lead to the development of a fatigue crack. Typical aluminum wings have very thin gauge aluminum aft of the main spar, and significant flexing may occur due to unsteady aerodynamic loads that are found in normal flight. Anywhere thin sheet metal is riveted to a stiff support has the potential for fatigue failure, therefore the wing inspection should carefully examine these areas.

Other areas where fatigue cracks are prevalent include the propeller bulkhead and spinner. These aluminum parts are subjected to cyclic loading from the engine and prop, and will frequently develop cracks found in the inspection. Figure 3-2-26 shows a typical fatigue crack on a propeller rear bulkhead.

Overstress. Aluminum sheet metal will effectively show an overstress situation by permanently deforming in some manner. If an airframe experiences an aerodynamic or ground handling overload, the aircraft will not necessarily fail catastrophically but may show damage in the deformation of the skin. Crippling or wrinkling of aluminum skins is a good sign that an aircraft has been overstressed and should be immediately grounded. A Monerai sailplane wing that has been overstressed is shown in Figure 3-2-27. Illuminating the surface of the wing by shining a light across the skin and looking for shadows and reflections will indicate abnormal bulging or wrinkling of the surface. Hidden damage to other parts of the structure should be assumed to exist in such a situation, such as deformation of seat rails which supported the pilot in the high load-factor maneuver.

Frequently in the design of a tube-spar aircraft, a liberal factor of safety is applied since the spar is really just a manufactured aluminum pipe, and available pipe sizes will dictate their usage in aircraft. The Kolb Aircraft Company has manufactured ultralights for 20 years, and has made extensive use of the tube spar design in several models of aircraft with a proven factor of safety. Company co-founder Dennis Souder took the Ultrastar up for an ultimate load test and intentionally pulled 6+ g's, failing the left wing rear spar (a smaller diameter aluminum tube) and having to deploy the ballistic parachute. The main spar did not fail, and was predicted to easily withstand a 7g load factor.

Now is a good time to mention the effect that holes have on the stress in structures, since many bolted aluminum structures are found in aircraft. A hole in a tube that receives bolt loads effectively raises the average stress by: 1.) decreasing the cross sectional area of the tube, and 2.) creating a stress concentration factor K which is inversely proportional to the diameter of the hole. As an example, consider a 1.0" x 0.065" tube with a 0.25" diameter hole carrying a bolt with a 1000 lb. load. The average stress in the tube away from the bolt hole will be:

$$\sigma = \frac{P}{A} = \frac{1000 \text{ lb}}{\frac{\pi}{4}\left(1^2 - 0.87^2\right)} = 5{,}240 \text{ p.s.i.}$$

σ = stress
P = load
A = cross-sectional area

Considering the reduced area around the hole, and a stress concentration factor of K = 2.5 based on the hole diameter, the stress near the hole becomes:

$$\sigma = \frac{1000 \text{ lb}}{\frac{\pi}{4}\left(1^2 - 0.87^2\right) - 2\left(0.25 \times 0.065\right)}(2.5) = 15{,}800 \text{ psi}$$

Since the stresses are approximately 3x higher around the hole, it is no wonder that these are the areas that fail first. Inspections of bolted airframes, mainly found on weight shift aircraft and powered parachutes, should always focus on the bolted joints. A typical failed joint is shown in Figure 3-2-28 showing some elongation of the hole and distortion of the paint around the hole. Note that powder-coated surfaces are more likely to show distortion than painted surfaces when overloaded because the

Figure 3-2-26. Fatigue crack on a propeller rear bulkhead due to cyclic loading.

Figure 3-2-27. Shadows and reflections show an overstressed condition on a sailplane wing.

coating is stiffer and more likely to separate from the base metal.

Checking an aluminum tube for overstress can be conducted by feeling the tube, or aiming a light down the length of the tube and looking for defects in the tube wall shape. Fittings attached to the tube will concentrate loads and may show signs of tearing or collapse in the tube wall if an overstress occurs. All fittings on an aluminum tube structure should be inspected for signs of hole elongation, free play or incorrect orientation, indicating that design loads have been exceeded.

In the case of weight shift aircraft, placing around 50 lbs. of pressure on the bottom lift wires of the wing will verify if there is any unwanted flexibility in the main lift structure. This can be accomplished by supporting the top wing while stepping on the lift wires. After placing a load on these wires, the rigging or tensions of wires on the aircraft should not have changed.

Another example of overstress occurs when a concentrated load is applied to an area that was not designed for the load resulting in a localized deformation of the material. Figure 3-2-29 shows a safety wire "eating" through an aluminum engine cooling shroud, which if left unchecked will completely destroy the shroud. With the steel safety wire being harder than aluminum, the bearing surface of the aluminum must be considerably larger to support the wire.

This is a good place to mention the stop drill, which is a small hole placed in a material that has begun cracking so that the crack will not propagate any further. Recall that a stress concentration factor around a hole is inversely proportional to its diameter. A stop drill places a relatively large hole at the tip of the crack which reduces the stress concentration factor and the stress that causes the crack to grow. Structures that are not designed to carry critical flight loads such windshields and shrouds are candidates for a stop drill operation. Cracking on load-bearing structural members require immediate repair as the integrity of the airframe has been compromised, resulting in a safety of flight issue.

Inspection of Wood Structures

At one time, the use of wood for aircraft was standard. With the advent of aluminum and modern assembly techniques, the use of wood declined. Recently, wood structures have made a noticeable comeback in the LSA and experimental areas. During the lean years, much of the expertise and knowledge of wood structures faded as well. There are some important aspects or inspecting wood structures that must be considered. The presence of moisture

Figure 3-2-28. A failed joint

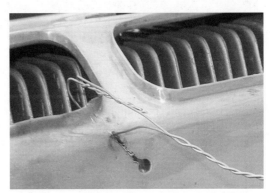
Figure 3-2-29. Overstressed safety wire pulling through a skin

Figure 3-2-30. Decay in a wood structure

in a wood structure will soon be followed by rot and deterioration of the area. Glue joints crack and fail but can be hard to find when the area is unloaded. Modern glues are far superior to the old casein glues and in many instances are stronger than the wood they bond.

When inspecting a wood wing, the following sources of deterioration and damage are most common:

Wood decay. When the moisture content of wood exceeds 20%, fungi will attack wood and cause its decay into a softer, non-structural form. When properly kiln dried, wood should have a moisture content of approximately 12%. Decayed wood exhibits softness, swelling if wet, excessive shrinkage if dry, as well as cracking and discoloration. Dark discoloration or

Figure 3-2-31. This structure has split along the grain line.

gray stains running along the grain will indicate a decay condition (Figure 3-2-30) on the previous page. If decay is detected, immediate attention is required to stop the source of the decay and then to repair or replace the damaged members.

Splitting. Splitting occurs along grain lines and usually happens as a result of cyclic dimensional changes caused by fluctuating moisture content. See Figure 3-2-31. Glue lines may lie at the root of splitting as the adjoining wood members create stresses at the interface, so in any wood inspection it is important to carefully examine glue joints for evidence of splitting.

Bond failure. A glue joint may fail simply because it was not manufactured properly, which is another reason to carefully inspect glue joints. As in a splitting failure, the load carrying capability of the member is seriously compromised and replacement will usually be necessary.

Finish failure. The failure of the outer protective coat on a wood member will selectively allow moisture to enter and begin the decay process. This type of failure may occur either because the outer coat has degraded in its environment, or it has been eroded by contact with another harder structure. In any case, it may be possible to fix the problem and arrest degradation before serious damage is done to the wood member because of the localized nature of this problem. Figure 3-2-32 shows a propeller tip that has deteriorated from loss of varnish due to the severe environment the propeller operates in.

Damage. Exceeding the crushing strength of wood is a common failure mode, usually caused by the over tightening of fittings mounted in

a wood structure. Other damage may occur from impact or aerodynamic loads that have exceeded design values. Inspecting for these is best done by looking for depressions or irregularities in the wood structure that would indicate some sort of abnormal loading.

Compression failure in wood is a common failure mode during an overstress situation, such as when a wing strikes the ground, or when the aircraft exceeds its rated design load. The top of the wing spars should be carefully examined for evidence of compression cracking, which would propagate perpendicular to the wood fiber direction.

Inspection methods for wood have been refined over the years as wood has been used for aircraft longer than any other structural material. The first condition for an adequate inspection is to remove as much of the covering material as possible for a clear view of the wood structure. Anytime an airframe is stripped of its covering, the underlying structure should be thoroughly examined since the airframe will be difficult to access after the covering is installed. Removable inspection plates typically cover inspection holes in a fabric wing, allowing an examination of critical parts of the airframe during a routine inspection.

Likely locations for wood deterioration should be noted in the inspection, such as areas where water may enter the structure, or be exposed to temperature extremes. Dark surfaces on the airframe that are in contact with wood parts will accelerate the degradation of adhesive strength and function. Wood members with fittings attached should be carefully inspected for cracks that may develop in the wood around the fitting, and are sometimes hidden under the fitting itself. Any evidence of rodents, insects or birds will require additional scrutiny in the affected area since harmful waste products and moisture will likely be found, and are detrimental to a wooden structure.

Since the wing spars carry the most critical loads in the aircraft, they should be inspected with the most intensity. Inspect for evidence of cracking near reinforcement plates and near the attachments of major load-carrying members such as the lift struts and wing root attach fittings. It is good practice to triple check these areas because their function is so critical. Figure 3-2-33 shows a nick in a wing spar that was created during spar construction, as evidenced by the varnish seen inside the cut. This defect is a perfect stress riser that needs to be addressed before the aircraft can fly again.

Some of the preferred inspection methods for wood structures are as follows:

Tapping. By tapping the wood structure with a screwdriver handle or plastic hammer, a sharp, solid sound should be heard. Any hollow, soft, or dull sound should be taken as an indication that damage may exist.

Probe. Areas in question can be examined with a sharp metal tool to determine if deterioration has occurred. By carefully probing the area, a detection of softness would indicate that damage may exist.

Prying. Bond joints can be evaluated by gently attempting to separate the bonded members. Any movement indicates that the bond has failed. A feeler gauge can be used to probe the joint as well. If the blade of the gauge enters the joint then further inspection is called for.

Odor. Musty or moldy smells indicate that deterioration is occurring in the wood structure.

Visual. Using a high-powered flashlight or borescope will greatly aid in the inspection of wood components. Similar to the composite inspection, any waviness in the surface when a beam of light is projected parallel to the surface in question can indicate a structural failure.

Figure 3-2-32. Finish failure

Figure 3-2-33. Nick on a wing spar, created during spar construction

Inspection of Fabric Surfaces

Fabric coverings for aircraft, as with most organic or synthetic woven materials, are subject to decomposition under UV radiation if they are not properly protected. This has required the regular replacement of aircraft envelopes which are not treated or coated with

Figure 3-2-34. Vertical ultralight fabric surfaces showing good color definition on vertical surfaces and faded color on the horizontal surfaces.

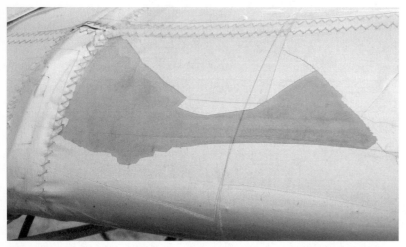

Figure 3-2-35. The loss of paint on this fabric wing was possibly caused by severe flexing or impact damage.

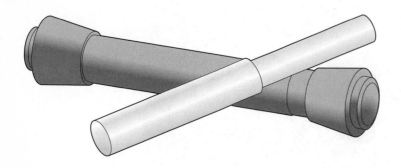

Figure 3-2-36. While not an approved inspection, a punch tester is a good first step in determining fabric strength.

a UV resistant barrier. For those coverings that are protected with a dope or paint, the condition of the surface needs to be maintained to prevent premature deterioration of the fabric.

In the ultralight community, UV degradation of a Dacron wing covering is usually the reason the covering must be replaced at regular intervals. Many ultralights lack a UV-resistant coating on the wing surface. The material may be dyed and this can serve as an excellent indication that the fabric strength might be degraded. Colored wings exposed to UV radiation will fade, and for those aircraft tied down outside for extended periods of time, the fading can become significant indicating significant strength degradation.

There have been documented in-flight failures of Dacron wings on ultralights due to UV degradation, and in one case, a post-accident pull test showed a strength of 25 to 40 lbs./in. for the faded wing material versus 120 to 130 lbs./in. for the unfaded material. In another report, during a walk-around inspection of an ultralight, a pilot tripped and fell into the wing and grabbed the leading edge to regain his balance, pushing his fingers right through the leading edge. Sometimes the most unsophisticated test technique will determine if a wing is safe or unairworthy. Figure 3-2-34 shows an ultralight control surface indicating strength degradation on the top side.

One ultralight manufacturer recommends a 400-hour or 2-year interval as the recommended replacement time for the wing covering. Adherence to the manufacturer's recommendations on maintenance of the wing envelope is critical for flight safety.

Inspection of the fabric covering should include deterioration as well as possible fit problems that may have originated when the envelope was originally installed on the wing. The tension of the fabric should not be so tight that it has begun to wear holes where it contacts the airframe. In the case of doped wings, excessive tension is the result of ongoing shrinkage of the fabric as the dope plasticizers migrate from the dope with age. The finish of the fabric may begin to crack as the coating becomes harder with age. In this case, the fabric remains intact as long as the protective coating remains in good condition. Figure 3-2-35 shows the loss of paint applied to a fabric wing, possibly after experiencing severe flexing or impact damage.

Loose fabric is caused by improper installation such as insufficient heat shrinkage or, for doped wings, too little doping material or the use of a poor quality of dope. The fabric may simply be installed with too much slack, or a structural failure inside the wing has reduced tension on the material. Fabric in advanced stages of UV deterioration can also show signs of looseness.

In weight shift aircraft, wear on the wing covering is most likely caused by the repeated set-up and break-down of the wing. Flex points near the leading edge and where the fabric is restricted from free movement by hardware will show accelerated wear. The batten pockets are also subject to wear as the battens are installed and removed, so these are areas that should be carefully inspected for holes or weakness, especially along the seams. Battens have become more sophisticated since the early hang glider designs, with locking leading edge tips that have internal mechanisms for activation from the trailing edge. In disassembly, these mechanisms should be inspected to make sure there are no broken or misaligned parts.

The Mylar insert in the leading edge of most weight shift wings must be carefully maintained so that creases do not turn into folds and bends that would adversely affect flight handling. Flight loads can be large enough to seriously distort the leading edge if there is weakness in the stiffening features, so a tactile inspection of the entire leading edge is necessary to identify localized weakness.

Fabric evaluation. In the evaluation of the quality of a fabric wing, the FAA recommends testing the fabric at every 100-hour/annual inspection for its load carrying capability. Tests commonly performed by mechanics, although not approved by the FAA in Part 43, include a punch test using a fabric testing tool that makes a small indentation or hole in the fabric and determines its strength from penetration depth, shown in Figure 3-2-36. The fabric tester is held perpendicular to the fabric surface and pressure is applied with a slight rotary action. When a certain depth is reached, a reading is taken from the device to determine the load carrying capacity of the fabric. This must be done on un-doped or unpainted fabric since any coating will create a false reading. Values are read as "pounds/in.," meaning if a strip of the fabric one-inch wide were fixed at one end and a weight applied to the other, the fabric would support the applied weight without failure.

A more accurate means of measuring fabric strength is to perform the load-carrying test directly. This can be accomplished by isolating an area of fabric and clamping the opposite ends so that the sample of fabric can be pulled. A calibrated scale attached to one set of the clamps will provide a direct load measurement on the material. As long as the fabric does not fail when the minimum pull strength is reached, the material should be safe. This measurement technique is easily performed on

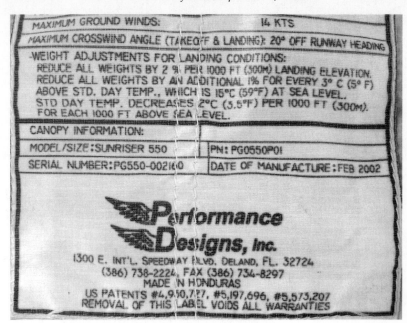

Figure 3-2-37. Data plate sewn into parachute fabric

balloons and powered parachutes where the fabric is unattached, but it may be impossible on a fixed wing design because of the installation and tight fit.

Tested fabric should come from areas that are suspected of having the most degradation, so that a worst case condition is evaluated. This would include areas that are exposed to sunlight, moisture and heat, with heat being significant on dark-colored surfaces exposed to the sun.

Inspection of Powered Parachute Canopies

Powered parachute canopies have a data plate sewn into the fabric that lists make, model, and the date of manufacture, shown in Figure 3-2-37. This information is critical in the inspection since it will help the inspector determine the age of the canopy. One popular manufacturer of canopies recommends a 500-hour replacement cycle, although canopies need to be inspected by the factory more frequently.

In addition to the annual condition inspection performed by the owner, most canopy manufacturers recommend that a 100-hour inspection be performed at the manufacturer, or by a master parachute rigger where more sophisticated inspection equipment is used. The cost of this inspection is usually not very expensive, making it low-cost insurance.

During the annual inspection, the canopy should be taken out of its storage bag and spread out on a clean floor, preferably large enough so that the entire canopy can be unfolded. Although this is ideal, an inspection can occur

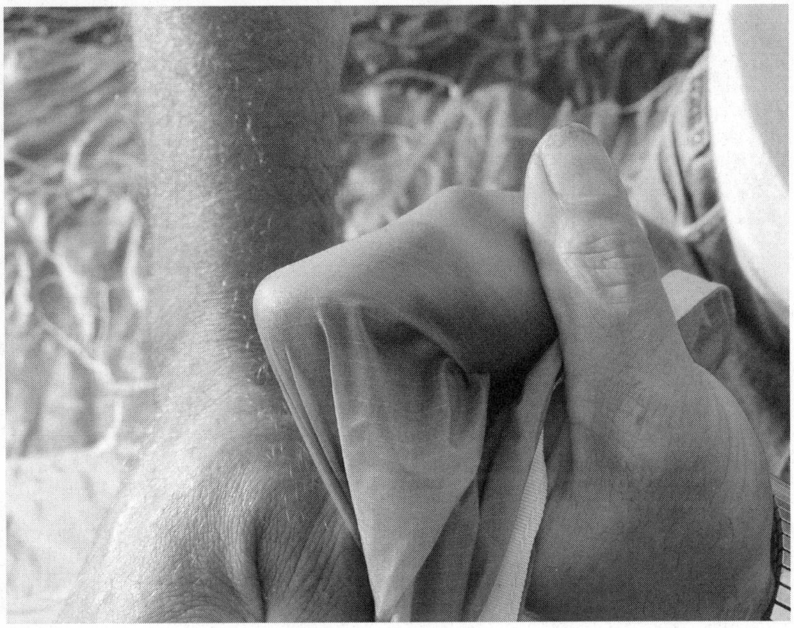

Figure 3-2-38. Strength testing the canopy

in a smaller area with careful accounting of the locations where the inspection has and has not occurred. The first test of the canopy is a qualitative strength test, where the inspector applies firm pressure with a finger or knuckle on an area of the top canopy while supporting the surrounding edges. A sliding motion of the finger or knuckle while applying pressure will stress the fabric and possibly reveal weakness by showing a small permanent deformation of the material, demonstrated in Figure 3-2-38. The top of the canopy is usually chosen for this test since it will be more susceptible to UV degradation than the bottom surface. Note that manufacturers rely on quantitative test data to determine canopy strength, and the technique described here is not endorsed by manufacturers for this reason. An obvious problem may be

Figure 3-2-39. Kevlar risers

revealed, but there may be other damage that only the manufacturer can find.

Some manufacturers may publish specific minimum tear strengths, and this can be evaluated as mentioned above, using clamps and a calibrated scale. Refer to the manufacturer's recommendations on conducting this test so that it yields accurate results.

Porosity. Porosity can be evaluated qualitatively by again locating a portion of the top canopy and holding a single layer up to one's mouth while inhaling, attempting to suck air through the material. Again, manufacturers do not endorse this technique as it cannot be used reliably to determine material degradation. Since most modern canopies are made of zero-porosity material, any detected flow indicates that the canopy should be immediately sent to the manufacturer for further testing.

Seams in the canopy should be checked by systematically moving from one side to the other and moving down each seam from leading edge to trailing edge while attempting to pull the seam apart with your hands. Again, the most general degradation should be found on the top canopy due to UV radiation, however, the bottom canopy has more concentrated loads where the lines are attached.

Inspection should continue at the line attach points, and then to the inside of the canopy. Ground debris will accumulate on the inside of the canopy during takeoff, and this has the effect of causing accelerated wear on the canopy because of its abrasive qualities. Debris that is found in the canopy can usually be shaken out by hand. The canopy dividers should be inspected for tears or loose seams.

Mildew and chemical burns. These are two additional forms of degradation that should be inspected for at this point. Mildew is evidenced by dark stains on the fabric from organic growth, and it may be unsightly but it will not degrade the fabric. Chemical burns originate from battery acid blown back by the propwash, or from fertilizer picked up in fields where launching takes place. Another source of chemical burns is from grasshoppers, which are acidic and leave a residue when trapped inside the canopy. Chemical burns are serious, and the manufacturer must determine if the canopy is safe for flight.

The risers should be carefully inspected as they carry the lift loads. Some powered parachutes are equipped with nylon risers that stretch, and the recommended replacement time for these is 100 hours. Be advised that nylon degrades in sunlight, similar to the canopy, and an inspection should focus on the part of the ris-

Figure 3-2-40. Quick links

ers exposed to direct sunlight. Other risers are constructed of Kevlar with a nylon jacket, as shown in Figure 3-2-39, allowing the Kevlar to be protected and serve as the main load carrying element. Steel cable risers are less likely to stretch, but in the inspection it is critical to check the lengths of the risers since a slight length offset will result in erratic inflation and behavior of the canopy.

From the risers, the parachute lines need to be systematically checked for wear, fraying or tangling. The lines are commonly attached to the risers using quick links, shown in Figure 3-2-40. These links are similar to the type available in a hardware store, but they have critical differences that should not be overlooked. Aircraft quality links are stainless steel and formed from a solid rod, so they have no mold lines or sharp edges that are found on the cheaper, more common cast links. Check the line around these links to make sure there is no abrasion on the line caused by a material defect. These links can be locked with a blue Locktite cement, but should always be checked to make sure they are tight and threaded to the limit of their travel.

In checking lines, it is always important to keep track of which lines have been inspected and which ones have not. Lines that have been inspected should systematically be placed off to one side away from the lines that have not been inspected. A tactile inspection should occur over the entire length of the line, checking for wear and fraying. Heat damage can occur if a line strikes the engine, and this can result in melting that significantly weakens the line.

Figure 3-2-41. Properly routed steering line

The steering lines should be inspected for any wear that may occur as the pass through rings or pulleys, and degradation due to UV exposure should also be checked. Figure 3-2-41 shows a steering line routed properly through guiding hardware to the trailing edge of the canopy.

SYSTEMS inspection

Section 1

Inspection of the Landing Gear

Jacking the Aircraft

A thorough inspection of the landing gear requires that the aircraft be jacked to relieve loads and allow a better view of the undercarriage. Reference should always be made to the manufacturer's recommendations on proper jacking procedure as structural components such as the skin are very weak when loaded transversely. Any loading into the airframe not approved by the manufacturer during jacking can damage the aircraft...do not compromise on the manufacturer's recommendations.

> **CAUTION:** *Extensive aircraft damage and serious personal injury have resulted from careless or improper jacking or hoisting procedures. As an added safety measure, all equipment should be inspected before use to determine the specific lifting capacity, proper functioning of safety devices, condition of pins and locks, and general serviceability.*

Inspection of the Suspension System

Landing gear design for light sport aircraft is not radically different from the landing gear design used in larger aircraft. The main types of gear that are used include:

- Cantilever spring-rectangular cross-section

Learning Objectives:

- *Inspection of the Landing Gear*
- *Inspection of the Controls and Control Surfaces*
- *Inspection of the Recovery Parachute System*
- *Cockpit Environment Inspection*
- *Electrical and Avionics Inspection*
- *Rigging and Assembly*

Left: This LSA has a combination of materials and systems that need inspection.

Figure 4-1-1. Cantilevered spring gear on a Cessna 150

Figure 4-1-3. Ultralight gear leg

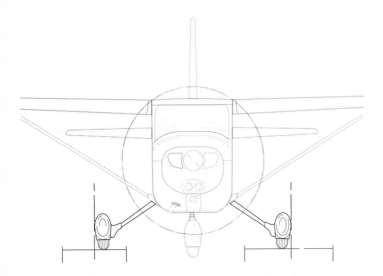

Figure 4-1-2. Cantilevered gear system mounting configuration

- Cantilever spring-circular cross section
- Oleo and spring-loaded struts
- Trailing link

These are all fixed-gear designs, since a retractable design is not allowed under LSA rules. Fairings are a common addition to fixed-gear aircraft to reduce drag, but they add complexity to the inspection since they usually obscure critically stressed areas.

Cantilevered spring-rectangular cross-section. This type of gear, shown in Figure 4-1-1, was patented in 1939 by the famous race plane builder and pilot, Steve Wittman. Wittman summarized the design of the gear in his patent as an "…especially simple, strong, and durable construction, and one in which the frontal area or head resistance is reduced to a minimum." By forming the spring at one end for mounting to the aircraft, and the other end for mounting to the wheel, this type of gear serves as

the supporting structure and the spring simultaneously. Its efficiency has seen its use on many general aviation aircraft, and now it has appeared in the LSA community as well.

Figure 4-1-2 shows the preferred mounting configuration for a cantilevered gear system, where added flexibility in the system is gained by supporting the leg so that it bends downward between the inside attach point and the bearing surface where the gear enters the airplane. Because of this added flexibility, wear on the gear leg may occur in the form of surface cracking and chafing where the weight of the airplane bears on the gear leg. This area will be difficult to inspect, but close examination of the contact area should be attempted to determine if freeplay has developed in the mounting system. At the inside end of the leg, attachment hardware may be subject to fatigue and should be examined for wear caused by flexing.

An overstress situation in a cantilever gear leg can be detected sometimes by observing the symmetry of the aircraft when it is parked on a level floor. Splayed legs or hardware that has been overstressed will result in landing gear that shows asymmetry or causes the airplane to lean to one side. The aircraft should be carefully observed head-on for this condition, and in some cases measurements may be necessary to verify that the gear has not been overstressed. Usually this type of landing gear has no provision for wheel alignment, so if the wheels are not tracking straight this may also be an indicator of an overstress situation.

There are typically three possible materials used in cantilever spring landing gear construction: high strength steel alloy, aluminum alloy, or composite. The metallic gears are more likely to show permanent deformation when overstressed, and the composite gears are more likely to suffer a sudden, brittle failure. Fiberglass and aluminum gear legs will be thicker than steel because of their lower strength and will tend to show more frictional wear, whereas a steel leg will tend to show more degradation due to corrosion.

Cantilevered spring-circular cross-section. This gear is common on many LSA aircraft as it is simple to manufacture and can be tailored to the weight of the aircraft by tapering on a lathe. Figure 4-1-3 shows an ultralight gear leg. Steel gear legs of this design may be tubular or solid, and frequently have stress concentration points where the gear is fitted into another tube or mounted to the airframe using bolts. These areas should be checked for an overstress situation, possibly aided by observing the aircraft as it sits on level ground to detect any asymmetry that would indicate material yielding.

Fiberglass gear legs are also common, shown in Figure 4-1-4, and these may reveal excessive loading by splintering or fracturing. Detection of these conditions may require the use of a magnifying glass, as the first indication of failure could be the appearance of a few glass fibers protruding from the leg. More obvious failure is shown in Figure 4-1-5 where a discolored longitudinal line appears near the bolt hole. Holes act as stress risers, and these areas should be carefully inspected since they not only raise stress but the landing loads are transferred to the airframe at these locations.

Oleo and spring-loaded struts. Another common gear design is the pneumatic-hydraulic system, where a piston pressurized by a gas such as nitrogen provides a low stiffness support while hydraulic fluid inside the cylinder acts as a damper as it is forced through a restricting orifice. See Figure 4-1-6. These systems provide a lightweight, smooth shock absorbing capability suited to aircraft and have

Figure 4-1-4. Fiberglass gear leg

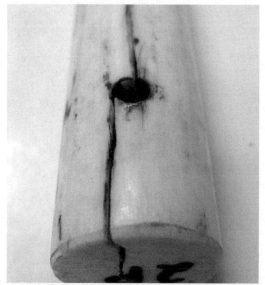

Figure 4-1-5. Discolored longitudinal crack near bolt hole of fiberglass landing gear

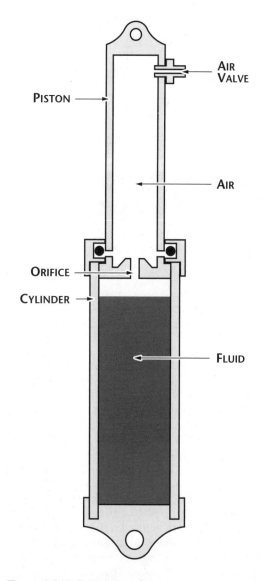

Figure 4-1-6. Strut internals

Figure 4-1-7. A typical aircraft oleo system

Figure 4-1-8. Scissors links or torque links keep the wheel aligned with the direction of travel.

been popular since the system was patented in 1915 by T. S. Duncan. Figure 4-1-7 shows a typical aircraft oleo system.

CAUTION: *Before servicing or disassembling any oleo strut, discharge all the air load. Many accidents have happened because the air load was not released prior to disassembly. Follow the manufacturer's recommendations at all times.*

Inspection of these systems should include a check of leaks of hydraulic fluid, which will give plenty of warning of a total system failure by weeping drops of fluid as the strut is actuated. The leaking can usually be attributed to a bad seal inside the strut or a defect in the strut itself. The strut piston is designed to a tight tolerance so that the high pressure system does not leak, and any small imperfection in the seal, or rusting, scoring and flaking of the strut piston will create a passage for fluid leakage. Again, slight leakage of hydraulic fluid does not indicate an immediate failure of the system, but maintenance should be planned to correct the situation.

Even if no leaks are detected, the surface finish of the strut piston should be carefully examined for wear or corrosion that may eventually cause a seal to fail. The piston surface is designed to be very smooth for proper operation, and any obvious defects should be addressed during maintenance.

The oleo struts on an aircraft are pressurized to an optimal value that translates to the desired extension when the aircraft is parked on level ground. The manufacturer usually specifies this strut extension when the aircraft is parked for a certain weight condition, such as empty or gross. During the inspection, this extension should be measured after the aircraft has been lowered from the jacked position. The strut piston should be cycled by carefully applying up and down pressure at a load-bearing part of the wing, which allows the aircraft to settle to the correct extension after a few bounces. This is a good time to assess the freedom of movement of the gear, where excessive binding on the strut seal or other restrictions will cause a jerky up and down motion. Carefully observe the operation of the linkages and piston to determine if maintenance is required.

Once the gear has settled to an average extension length this distance is measured and compared to the manufacturer's recommendations. If the strut is pressurized with air instead of nitrogen, it will be more susceptible to temperature effects and may need to have a correction applied.

Figure 4-1-9. Trailing link suspension

Service the strut as specified by the manufacturer if the extended length is not correct.

Scissors links, or torque links, commonly accompany an oleo gear system to keep the wheels aligned with the direction of travel. These links provide a resistance to rotation about the axis of the oleo piston but do not prevent motion up and down, the desired action of the gear leg. See Figure 4-1-8. Lubrication as specified by the manufacturer should be present on the link joints, and they should be checked for free-play which should not exceed a published value. The links should be inspected for cracks due to fatigue or overstress loading, a condition that may be evident in taxi when the airplane pulls to one side when - are applied.

Spring-loaded struts are cheaper and easier to maintain than oleo struts, and have found recent popularity in the mountain bike industry and in automotive cargo hatch applications. They outwardly appear as an oleo gear except that there is no gas pressurization used to carry the load. An internal spring carries the gear loads, and in some cases a piston will force air or hydraulic fluid through an orifice to provide some measure of damping. This gear design can wear significantly since there is usually a tight tolerance between the telescoping tube and the spring, resulting in metal-to-metal contact. Evidence of hydraulic fluid or particles of metal would indicate a faulty system.

Trailing link suspension. Dating back to 1940, the trailing link suspension first found common application in the Ercoupe, an aircraft designed by legendary aeronautical engineer Fred Weick. A typical system is shown in Figure 4-1-9. The trailing link suspension is a simple design comprised of a pivoting "trailing link" arm that guides the wheel in an arc to absorb energy, while maintaining directional orientation. A spring or stack of rubber bushings ("doughnuts") are mounted to the end of the trailing link and provide stiffness to the system. Rubber bushings will tend to degrade with time, and may sag or get stiff which will cause a difference in suspension height or shock response. These should be inspected for distortion and hardness that would indicate a worn bushing. Figure 4-1-10 shows bushings that are cracking, mainly due to age.

Trailing link suspensions frequently use metallic bushings at the pivoting joints, and these should be checked for excessive wear, especially when the aircraft is operated from unimproved or gravel runways. Excessive grease on landing gear bushings will attract dirt and dust which accelerates wear by abrading the bushing surfaces. Therefore, it is important that the gear components be clean without excessive oil or grease on the link members.

Inspection of the Wheels and Bearings

The wheels (or rims) used on LSA vary from the types found on small aircraft certified under Part 23, to agricultural or utility wheels found in the garage. Figure 4-1-11 shows one type of wheel and tire used on LSAs. Aircraft-grade wheels are designed with weight in mind, so they are usually cast aluminum or magnesium, or spun aluminum construction. These materials can be dented and bent in the abusive

Figure 4-1-10. Cracked rubber suspension bushings.

Figure 4-1-11. One type of wheel and tire used on LSAs.

Figure 4-1-12. Unsealed ball bearings on utility wheel with a grease fitting

Figure 4-1-13. Sealed ball bearing

landing environment, and in the case of cast wheels, shattering is possible. Dented or bent wheels may hold air and function properly, but they are weakened and should be replaced as soon as practicable.

> **CAUTION:** *Before removing any split or two-part wheel from the axle of the aircraft it is advisable to completely deflate the tire first. Should any of the bolts or retainers fail, the only thing holding the wheel together would be the axle nut. A number of people have been injured when the wheel suddenly exploded when the last couple of threads of the axle stripped off under pressure.*

In general, wheels should be inspected for cracks, corrosion, dents, distortion, and faulty bearings in accordance with the manufacturer's service information. Bolt holes in two-piece wheels, and the bolts and nuts used in assembly should be inspected for deformation and wear. The torque values used in two-piece wheel assemblies are critical to the proper operation of the wheel, and this should be checked with

the manufacturer's recommendation when the wheel is reassembled.

Steel one-piece wheels commonly labeled as utility wheels are subject to the same kinds of abuse as aircraft wheels, but may be more forgiving in impact damage since they will tend to yield as opposed to fracturing. An inspection of a steel wheel should include seams and welds where corrosion may be more prevalent, and the outer rim should be inspected for trueness. Corrosion should also be inspected around holes and other stressed areas.

Bearings on LSA wheels are usually roller or ball, sealed or unsealed. Aircraft wheels frequently use roller bearings that must be disassembled, cleaned and inspected and then repacked with grease during maintenance. Using a 10x magnifier, the outer and inner races of the roller bearing should be inspected for scoring, pitting and heat damage. The cage that holds the rollers should be inspected for cracks and other defects that may cause it to disintegrate during operation. Never dry bearings that have been cleaned out by using high pressure air to spin the bearing. This may cause a worn bearing to come apart explosively, causing injury to nearby persons.

Ball bearings that are unsealed are commonly found on utility wheels with a grease fitting mounted to the wheel hub, as shown in Figure 4-1-12. These bearings are usually pressed into the wheel as an assembly, so the inspection may be limited to spinning the wheel and listening for a grinding or roaring sound that would indicate pitted and worn bearings. These bearings should operate smoothly and quietly when properly maintained. Excess grease that is forced out of the bearing during service should be removed so that dirt and debris are not attracted to the bearing area. Since the bearing is an integral part of the wheel, maintenance is limited to replacement of the entire wheel assembly.

Sealed bearings are becoming more common on aircraft, as shown in Figure 4-1-13. They are typically found on cast alloy wheels specifically designed for aircraft, and these bearings are usually replaceable if they wear out. The inspection of these bearings is also limited to spinning the wheel and listening for a roaring or grinding sound. Since there is no lubricant to worry about, a noisy sealed bearing can only be fixed by replacing it with a new part.

Inspection of the Tires

A schematic of a typical aircraft tire is shown in Figure 4-1-14. Tires for aircraft are optimized to keep the aircraft tracking straight and provide good braking action on wet or dry surfaces.

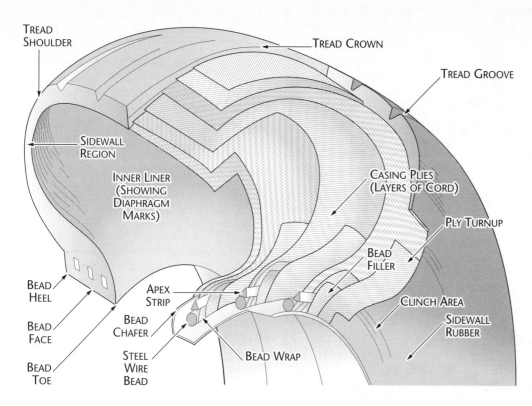

Figure 4-1-14. Schematic of a typical bias aircraft tire

Although there isn't a lot of mileage put on them in a given year, they tend to wear quickly because of landing loads, where the tire transitions from a standstill to full rotational speed in a fraction of a second. Simply wearing the tread down is the most common form of tire wear, and this is evaluated by observing the amount of tread left on the tire. If the tire does not have a wear indicator then the maximum allowable wear is when the bottom of the tread groove becomes flush with the tire surface. As with automotive tires, if the tire has a wear indicator then the acceptable amount of wear is to the top of the indicator and not beyond it.

Normal landing loads will wear a tire evenly, but certain conditions may result in very uneven wear of the tread. Skidding caused by a locked wheel will rapidly wear the tread at a single place, and the tire should be examined completely for a flat spot. Transitioning from ice to pavement and hydroplaning both contribute to this type of wear, which should be considered serious if the tire belts are exposed.

There are several sources of wear beyond simple landing loads. Misalignment, under- or overpressure, UV degradation and ozone all will contribute to accelerated wear. Examples are shown in Figure 4-1-15. The detection of these conditions is an indication that maintenance should address the cause of the problem, such as a realignment of the gear or proper tire inflation pressure and not just change the tires.

Tires should be carefully inspected for foreign object debris (FOD) damage, which can penetrate the tread area but not damage the tire. In these cases, damage may be imminent if the object is not removed immediately. If the object has penetrated the tire carcass it may not cause a leak, but removal will cause rapid deflation. Care should be taken to never remove the object with the tire inflated, as it may be ejected with enough force while being removed to cause an injury. Instead, mark the location of the object with a piece of chalk or crayon, deflate the tire and then remove the foreign object. FOD damage can include the

Figure 4-1-15. Examples of tire wear beyond simple landing loads

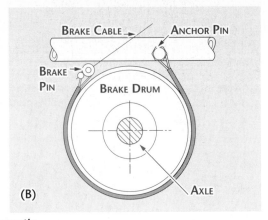

Figure 4-1-16 (A)Band brake (B) and band brake schematic

Figure 4-1-17. Drum brake

work by developing friction between the moving wheel and the fixed frame, applied through a brake pad or shoe onto a rotor or drum.

Mechanical brakes have cables that should be inspected for kinks, fraying and corrosion where the cable is exposed. A band brake is shown in Figure 4-1-16. Figure 4-1-17 shows a drum brake. A functional check should be made with the wheel off of the ground to verify the sensitivity of the system and indicate any needed adjustment in cable length.

Hydraulic brake systems can be of the type commonly found on general aviation aircraft, such as the Cleveland brake shown in Figure 4-1-18, or a mechanical/hydraulic brake shown in Figure 4-1-19 that is used on mountain bikes. The use of both a mechanical cable and a hydraulic system is a novel design, and an inspection needs to look at both systems. Matco has developed several, novel new brake designs for aircraft including the internal caliper brake seen in Figure 4-1-20 B. A schematic of the typical hydraulic brake caliper is shown in Figure 4-1-21. The anchor bolts, or guide pins should be inspected for freedom of movement in the torque plate so that the caliper self-

Figure 4-1-18. Cleveland brake

most unusual items, such as one documented case of a piece of aluminum tape discarded during paint stripping that penetrated the tire carcass and caused a flat tire

Inspection of the Brakes

Brake systems on LSA range from conventional aircraft systems to novel innovations such as the application of mountain bike brakes. Regardless of the origin of the brake, they all

Figure 4-1-19. Mechanical/hydraulic brake like those used on mountain bikes.

centers on the rotor. A close-up of these pins is shown in Figure 4-1-20 A.

Hydraulic brakes require a fluid line from the wheel cylinder to the master cylinder, with a reservoir mounted at a high point in the system, shown in Figure 4-1-22. The entire system should be checked for leaks, especially around pistons and cylinders. Flexible hoses should be replaced when any hardness, or inflexibility caused by

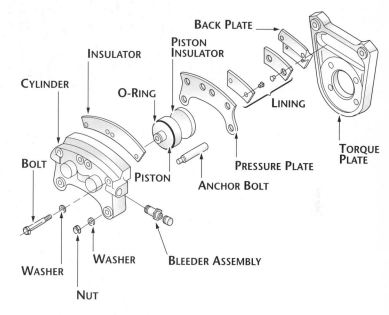

Figure 4-1-20. (A) Brake caliper anchor bolt or pin. (B) An internal caliper brake

Figure 4-1-21. Exploded view of Cleveland brake caliper design

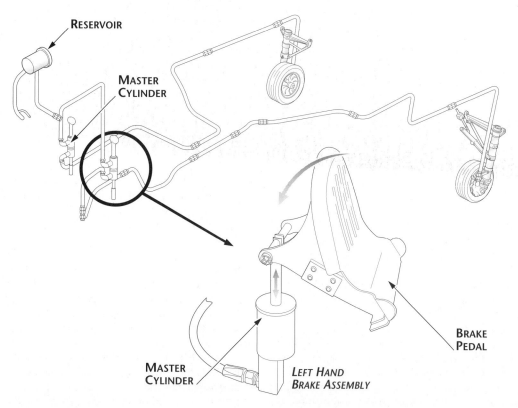

Figure 4-1-22. This type of hydraulic brake has a reservoir mounted at a high point in the system.

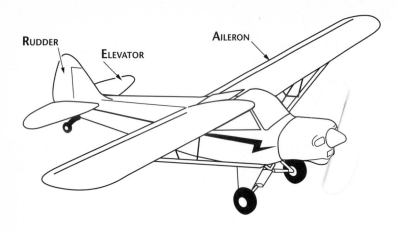

Figure 4-2-1. Aerodynamic control surfaces

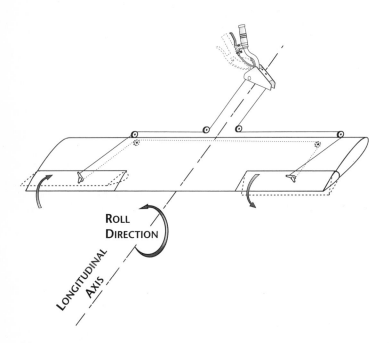

Figure 4-2-2. Ailerons, mounted on the outboard section of the wings, control roll by deflecting in opposite directions causing the wings to generate a differential lift.

heat and age, or fraying of the braided cover are found during the inspection. Metal tubing that is found to have any nicks, cuts, dents, abrasion, or deformation beyond approved limits should also be replaced or repaired. The reservoir should be checked for the proper level and type of hydraulic fluid, as specified by the manufacturer. Automotive brake fluid is not compatible with red Mil–H- 5606 hydraulic fluid used in most aircraft systems.

Another important part of the brake system inspection is the condition of the pads or shoes, and the rotor or drum. They should be checked against the manufacturer's allowable limits. Pads and shoes that meet the wear requirement should be checked for cracks or chipped edges

that will limit their effectiveness and require replacement. Rotors can become warped from heat build-up during braking, and they may become pitted and severely rusted in a moist environment when they are not used frequently. With the advent of mountain bike technology finding its way into LSA, replacement of these components has become a cheap and easy option as opposed to remanufactured products.

Section 2

Inspection of the Controls and Control Surfaces

Controls and control surfaces on fixed wing aircraft include the pilot controls and aerodynamic surfaces needed for roll, pitch and yaw motion, as well as lift augmentation devices such as flaps or spoilers. A planform view of typical aerodynamic control surfaces is shown in Figure 4-2-1. The ailerons, mounted on the outboard section of the wings, control roll by deflecting in opposite directions, causing the wings to generate a differential lift. When an aileron is deflected upward, the total lift on the wing is decreased while the downward deflecting aileron increases lift. The net effect is to cause the airplane to roll, shown in Figure 4-2-2. The pilot usually controls the ailerons through a stick or wheel inside the cockpit, where lateral motion of the control actuates the control surfaces. In the interest of keeping the cockpit simple and optimizing space, some LSA have a single control stick mounted between the pilot and passenger, as shown in Figure 4-2-3. Note that the aircraft brake control is also simplified by mounting on the stick as well.

The elevator is the control surface mounted on the horizontal stabilizer and acts to pitch the aircraft up and down when the control stick or wheel is moved fore and aft. As the elevator moves, it changes the angle of attack of the air on the tail that increases or decreases its aerodynamic force, causing the airplane to pitch up or down. Figure 4-2-4 shows the aerodynamic force vector generated on the tail as the elevator is deflected.

The rudder provides a yawing motion (left and right around the vertical axis) and is most frequently used to yaw the aircraft when coordinating turns and aligning the aircraft with the runway for landing. Turn coordination is aided with the rudder to counteract the adverse yaw created by the ailerons. Since drag is associated with lift, a downward deflected aileron will generate more drag than an upward deflected aileron because of the lift differential. This tends to yaw the airplane in the opposite direction of the turn, an action can be corrected with the rudder for proper turn coordination. Adverse yaw can also corrected by using aileron design features, like Frise ailerons or differential aileron control. Frise ailerons have a hinge point behind the leading edge of the control which allows the nose of the up aileron to dip below the bottom of the wing creating a drag component that is equal to the drag created by the down aileron. The use of differential aileron travel, is another way of controlling adverse yaw. In this system when the aileron is deflected up the travel is greater than the down travel, this creates more drag on the wing with the up aileron.

On fixed wing aircraft, controls may be actuated by push rods or cables that extend from the cockpit to the surfaces that deflect on the wing and tail. As a preliminary check of the controls, the stick or wheel should be operated over its full range of motion with a "stirring" motion. There should be no binding or unusual noises in the cockpit or outside the airplane. This check should be done whenever work is performed in the area near the controls, or on the controls themselves, to ensure that nothing has moved or created an obstacle to freedom of motion. The same full motion travel test should be performed with the rudder as well.

Positive control check. This is a phrase used to indicate a check of the controls while a resisting load is applied to the control surfaces. For years the glider community has implemented the positive control check as a means to verify proper connections of the controls after the wings and tail surfaces are hooked up when the glider is assembled. In performing this check, any abnormal motion or sounds should be investigated as the controls are moved through their full range. Keep in mind that pressure on the control surfaces with and against the direction of motion as the stick or wheel is moved left and right or fore and aft is important to detect for abnormalities in the linkages. Obviously this check requires two people, with one person carefully applying a distributed pressure on the control surface while the controls are actuated from the cockpit. The proper technique is shown in Figure 4-2-5.

A pushrod control system is shown in Figure 4-2-6, next page. The use of rod-end bearings is common in this arrangement, and the inspection should focus on the threaded area of the bearings for cracks or yielding caused by overstress. Even a slight bend in the threaded portion of the bearing can result in a failure as cyclic loads are applied with time. Rod-end bearings may require a light lubricant as specified by the manufacturer. Lubrication with the wrong type of material can actually attract dirt to the area, which will result in accelerated wear of the bearing surface. The lack of a lubricant will create metal-to-metal contact and

Figure 4-2-3. A control stick between pilot and passenger seats optimizes space in the cockpit.

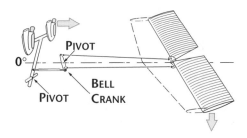

Figure 4-2-4. Aerodynamic vector force generated on the tail as the elevator is deflected.

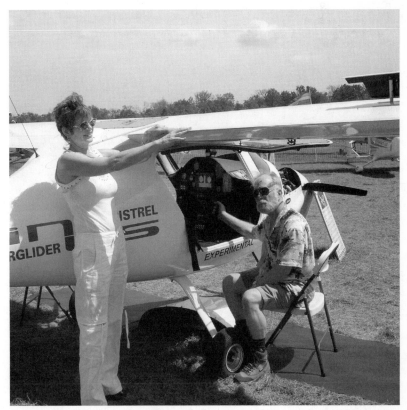

Figure 4-2-5. Positive control check

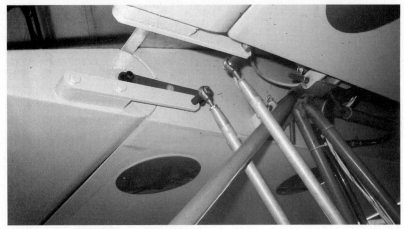

Figure 4-2-6. Pushrod control system

Figure 4-2-7. Cable system

the bearings will wear out prematurely. Each bearing should be rotated to the extent allowed to evaluate the play in the bearing surface, and replacement should occur if the free play is larger than recommended values. Conversely, if binding occurs, the bearing may be seized and will require replacement.

A cable control system is shown in Figure 4-2-7. Several components of a typical cable system are shown in Figure 4-2-8. The turnbuckle is equipped with a locking wire, or pin, that prevents rotation once the proper cable tension has been set. Turnbuckles should be inspected for the locking wire and straightness of the ends that screw into the barrel. Like the rod-end bearing, any bends at this point can lead to sudden failure of the system.

The thimble is the stainless steel cable guide around the end of the cable entering the turn-buckle, used to prevent excessive cable wear around terminal locations. Thimbles can slide off of the cable if they are not mounted tightly during cable swaging, and so they should be inspected to ensure proper routing.

The copper Nicopress collars shown in Figure 4-2-8 are swaged using the Nicopress tool, and they should show the telltale pattern of being properly squeezed or swaged. If a swage appears to be accomplished with pliers or some other inferior tool, the swage must be replaced. The integrity of the swages is the weak link in a cable system, and its strength is very important to the whole system. As a note, most of the load of swaged joint is carried by the collar closest to the loop of the cable, and the second swage is really just to terminate the end of the cable.

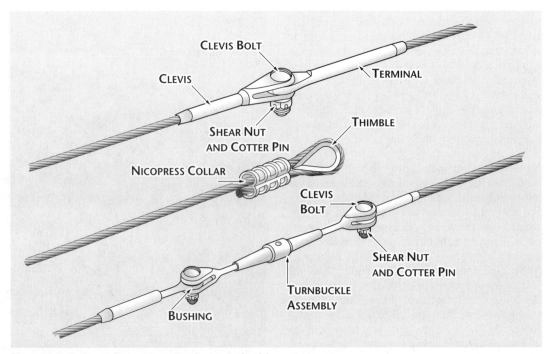

Figure 4-2-8. Several components of a typical cable system.

Figure 4-2-9. Marine hardware used in a control system

Figure 4-2-10. Aircraft grade pulley

Therefore, the swage nearest the cable loop should be carefully inspected.

Pulleys are usually associated with cable control systems, and on LSA they may appear as marine hardware (Figure 4-2-9) or more commonly as fiber reinforced aircraft grade pulleys as seen in Figure 4-2-10. Freedom of motion should be checked, and proper lubrication should be applied so that the pulley will not be subject to binding. A flat spot will eventually develop on a stuck pulley causing the cable to rub over it. This will prevent the smooth operation of the system and a possibility of the controls binding. Pulleys should be observed while operating the system to detect any possible binding that may occur. The cable should not be lubricated where it contacts the pulley in order to ensure that a dry friction contact is made.

The aerodynamic surfaces of an aircraft control system should be checked for smoothness of operation without binding, as an extension of the positive control check. Hinges should be inspected and lubricated as required by the manufacturer.

Aerodynamic surfaces on an aircraft are frequently balanced to prevent a structural/aerodynamic instability called flutter from occurring. It is vitally important that all balance weights on control surfaces be mounted securely to the control surface. Any slippage in the bolted connection of a balance weight can create a flutter in the surface as through it were not balanced.

Control surfaces tend to be some of the weaker structures on an airframe, and they should be carefully inspected for broken ribs, fabric tears, delaminations (composites) and corrosion (aluminum). Aerodynamic and structural interactions with a damaged control surface can result in instabilities that may result in the surface coming apart from the aircraft.

Powered parachutes have a unique control system, using steering lines actuated by a steering bar to affect turning. Figure 4-2-11 shows a pilot applying pressure to the left steering bar with his foot which puts tension on the left steering line. Figure 4-2-12 shows the left side of the canopy, with the fore and aft risers supporting the weight of the aircraft while the steering line, attached to the trailing edge of the canopy, deflects the trailing edge down during actuation. This increases drag on the

Figure 4-2-11. The steering bar of a powered parachute being pushed down to turn left.

Figure 4-2-12. The left side of the canopy being deflected down, causing a turn to the left.

Figure 4-2-13. Steering line properly connected to the trailing edge of the canopy.

affected side of the canopy, causing the aircraft to turn in that direction.

An inspection of this control system should include the integrity of the steering line, proper length during flight, and any wear or abrasion that may occur on the line as it passes through guides and pulleys. The steering line properly connected to the trailing edge of the canopy should be inspected for security (Figure 4-2-13), next page, and that all trailing edge connections are of the correct length.

Weight shift trikes, as the name suggests, use weight shift for control so there are no aerodynamic controls on this type of LSA. The airframe inspection should include the main pivot joint and full control motion of the wing, which is adequate to evaluate the aircraft control system.

Section 3

Inspection of the Recovery Parachute System

The recovery parachute has become a familiar addition to aircraft in recent years, following the lead of the hang glider and ultralight communities which have used airframe recovery parachutes since the 1970's. Many lives have been saved by these devices, which are deployed in the event that the pilot cannot make a safe landing. It is necessary to inspect the whole system for any abnormalities that may restrict proper parachute deployment, and to inspect the airframe attachment hardware to ensure that once the chute is deployed, a safe descent will be made.

Recovery parachute systems are typically deployed in one of five ways:

Hand deployment. In a hand deployed system, the parachute is stored within the pilot's reach so that in an emergency, it can be grabbed and thrown overboard. This system can be deployed in about five seconds and is suited to lighter aircraft since the parachute size is restricted.

Spring activated drogue chute. This system is usually mounted in free air so that when it is triggered, a drogue chute is pushed out by the spring that then pulls the main chute out. Average deployment time is three to five seconds.

The ballistic drogue gun system. In this system, a small cannon fires a slug that is attached to the top of the parachute, pulling the parachute out of its canister as the slug travels away from the aircraft. The deployment time is under two seconds, but the recoil can be as high as 2,000 to 3,000 lbs as the parachute inflates.

The rocket deployed parachute system. A small solid fuel rocket is launched in this system, pulling the parachute out with 40 to 100 lbs of thrust as it burns for about one second. This system has become the most popular method of deployment, in part due to the fact that the rocket motor can be aimed separately from the parachute canister. This allows more options when placing the canister in the airframe. The deployment of these systems is relatively smooth and the danger of ignition is low. The rocket motor burns for less than 1 second and the exhaust is composed of inert gasses that do not support combustion. Figure 4-3-1 shows a cutaway view of a rocket launched system, with the rocket and firing mechanism located at the top of the parachute canister.

Mortar launched system. The mortar launched system consists of a high pressure gas generator that feeds a low pressure cylinder containing the parachute. As pressure builds, the parachute if forced out of the container at a high velocity, such as 100 ft./sec. Opening time is less than two seconds.

Inspecting these systems is relatively easy, since the more complicated operating parts are usually off limits for airplane owners and can only be accessed by the manufacturer.

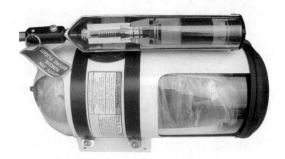

Figure 4-3-1. Cutaway of a rocket launched parachute system

CAUTION: *Accidental activation of the firing device of any these systems when the aircraft is on the ground or in a hangar can result in serious injury to anyone nearby. The activation mechanism should always be safe-tied when the aircraft is not in flight.*

The mounting system consists of a relatively low-force system that holds the parachute or container to the airframe. A high-force mount is used where the parachute main riser is attached to the airframe. A schematic of a typical mounting system is shown in Figure 4-3-2 and Figure 4-3-3 shows a typical parachute recovery instal-

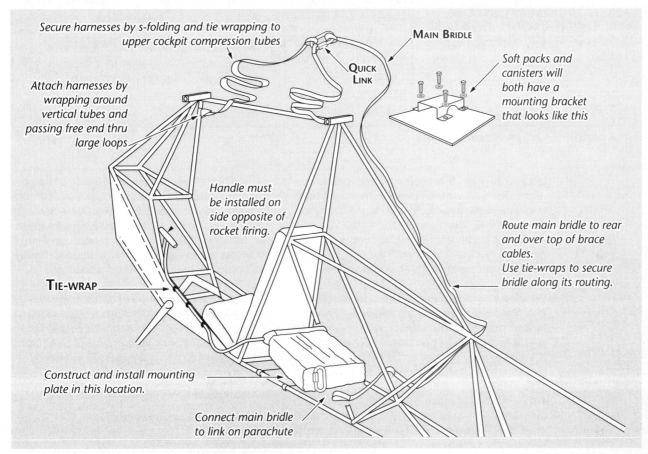

Secure harnesses by s-folding and tie wrapping to upper cockpit compression tubes

MAIN BRIDLE

QUICK LINK

Soft packs and canisters will both have a mounting bracket that looks like this

Attach harnesses by wrapping around vertical tubes and passing free end thru large loops

Handle must be installed on side opposite of rocket firing.

Route main bridle to rear and over top of brace cables.
Use tie-wraps to secure bridle along its routing.

TIE-WRAP

Construct and install mounting plate in this location.

Connect main bridle to link on parachute

Figure 4-3-2. A schematic of a typical mounting system

Figure 4-3-3. Typical parachute recovery installation

WARNING	BRS-5	Model: UL2
NEVER POINT CHUTE DISCHARGE TOWARD ANYONE AT ANYTIME- ACCIDENTAL DISCHARGE CAN CAUSE DEAH OR SERIOUS INJURY. TREAT IT LIKE A LOADED GUN. IF YOU ARE NOT THE ORIGINAL OWNER OF THIS BRS UNIT, CONTACT BRS INC. FOR PERTINENT PRODUCT ADVISORIES. BRS INC. 300 AIRPORT RD. SOUTH ST. PAUL, MN 55075 USA	TESTING HAS SHOWN HIS PARACHUTE TO BE LIMITED TO AIRCRAFT GROSS WEIGHTS UNDER 750 LBS (340 KG), AT DEPLOYMENT SPEEDS UNDER 100 MPH (160 KM/H). EXCEEDING THESE LIMITATIONS, OR USING IMPROPER INSTALLATION, MAY CAUSE DEPLOYMENT FAILURE AND DEATH OR SERIOUS INJURY TO OCCUPANTS. US PATENT PROTECTED COMPONENTS, PATENTS 4,863,119 & 4,607,814 SN:1 BRS-5 750 INERT/CUT AWAY BUILT: 07/03 25 LBS. 11OZ DO NO USE AFTER: 07/09	

Figure 4-3-4. A parachute recovery system data plate

lation. Both of these attachment points are important and require close inspection, however, where the parachute is attached to the airframe is by far the more critical of the two. The reinforced bridle and associated hardware must have a very close inspection since they will be subject to very high loads at a critical time.

When any of the ballistic systems are deployed, two shocks will be felt by the pilot. The first "snatch force" is the inertia of the deployed components reacting on the bridle as all slack is taken out of the system. The second shock is the resistance of the parachute in the relatively high velocity air, causing a deceleration of the aircraft that may reach 10g. For this reason, the mounting system of the bridle to the airframe must be designed to withstand a 10g load, while keeping the occupants inside the airplane. The bridle is typically routed to high load bearing points on the airframe, and in some cases to the occupants' harnesses to ensure a safe descent.

An inspection of the recovery system should include a close examination of the bridle and its routing to ensure it will not become entangled in the airframe during deployment. Tie wraps that are used to hold the bridle in place will degrade in sunlight, and these should be replaced if they show signs of degradation. For rocket launched systems, the position of the rocket launcher should be checked to ensure a clean deployment path away from the airframe. This includes the entire system: the rocket is attached to the parachute via steel lanyards, and the parachute is attached to the airframe via the bridle. None of these components should contact the airframe during deployment.

The red handle that activates the recovery system, the housing, and the cable guide that protects the cable to the firing pins makes up the activation system. The cable guide should not have kinks or coils in it that would restrict

motion of the trigger cable, and a careful inspection should include mounting tie wraps that may be become loose or degraded with time. Since 30 to 40 lbs. pull force is necessary for deployment, the handle housing and its mounting should be inspected to ensure it will withstand higher loads and not break free when activated.

CAUTION: *Do not check the cable for freedom of movement while it is connected to the firing mechanism. Failure to disconnect the cable from the firing mechanism will result in the parachute being deployed. Remember to re-connect the cable after the inspection.*

• Parachute

• Explosives or rocket fuel

• Canister condition

Parachutes. Parachutes need to be inspected and repacked on a calendar basis. The date of the last repack or the original date is either indicated directly on the unit data plate (as above), or must be determined from the date of manufacture and any maintenance logbook entries. Additionally, the data plate on a parachute canister will include the weight, and this can be important information if the owner suspects that water has entered the canister. (See Figure 4-3-4). By weighing the canister, any water or other contaminant will be detected by its increased weight. If this is the case, the canister should be sent back to the manufacturer for service.

Explosives or rocket fuel. Many of the older rocket motors and explosive devices have a service life that requires them to be returned to the manufacturer for inspection and service. The service life of these devices is listed on the data plate and in the maintenance records for the aircraft.

Since the shipping of explosives is a difficult process, many of the manufacturers have made devices that have a longer service life. Once that time period has expired, the unit can be disposed of in accordance with the manufacturers recommendation and a new unit installed.

Canister condition. The parachute canister should be inspected for any type of damage that may affect how the parachute deploys. This includes dents and crushing of the container itself. Units that are installed close to the ground are more susceptible to damage from rocks and debris during landing and takeoffs than those mounted higher on the airframe. Any evidence that water has been allowed to enter the canister should be taken very seriously. If a weight check shows an increase in weight then the canister must be replaced since this is evidence of some form of contamination inside the container.

Additional inspection items include:

Vibration-related problems. Two stroke cycle engines can produce vibrations that will loosen many of the components of the recovery system. All the bolts and nuts that are used to attach the system to the airframe should be carefully inspected for correct torque values. All safeties should also be checked for proper condition. Band clamps are particularly prone to shifting, which can allow the whole system to rotate and change the orientation of the ballistic portion of the system.

Ultraviolet degradation. Sunlight is one of the most problematic sources of ultraviolet light. It is responsible for the degradation of the materials used in the parachute recovery systems. The containers are closed with a plastic cap that should be replaced if continuous exposure has caused any damage or cracking. Any light that is allowed to enter the container can cause damage to the fabric of the canopy. The bridles

are usually sheathed to protect them from UV radiation, but should be inspected for any sign of damage caused by sunlight.

Many of the lines are secured with tie wraps that become hard and brittle after being exposed to sunlight for an extended period. These need to be replaced on a periodic basis so that they do not break during flight and create entanglement problems.

Corrosion. Undetected, corrosion can dangerously weaken a critical part in the recovery system that then is only detected when it breaks during an emergency. All the metal parts in the system that withstand the high forces generated during a parachute deployment should be inspected and replaced when any corrosion is present.

Section 4
Cockpit Environment Inspection

The cockpit of an aircraft is where the pilot's attention is focused during flight, and therefore should be inspected carefully for any potential problems. The cockpit is where the aircraft is controlled, the airspeed is monitored and the engine instruments are mounted. Any communication and navigation devices are also located here within easy reach of the pilot.

As with other aspects of LSA, the variation from one aircraft cockpit to another is large. Transitional ultralights that currently have a sparse instrument panel with a few switches marked with a felt-tipped pen (Figure 4-4-1)

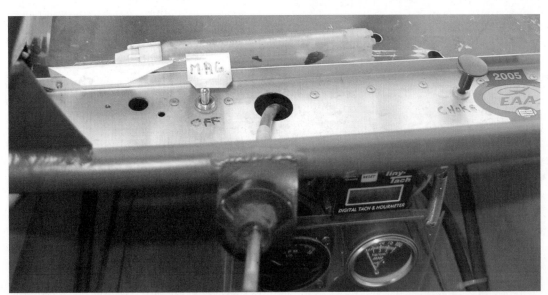

Figure 4-4-1. In order to meet a minimum level of functionality, transitional ultralights with few switches will probably have to be replacarded.

Figure 4-4-2. An LSA cockpit equipped with the latest navigational technology similar to that in a glass cockpit aircraft.

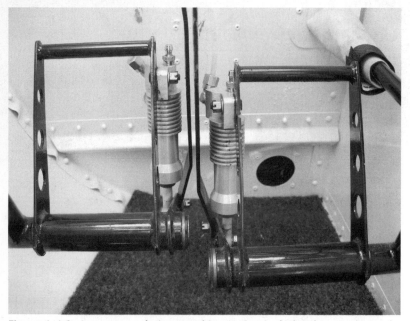

Figure 4-4-3. A proper cockpit control inspection includes the area around the rudder pedals.

Figure 4-4-4. Many LSA control systems will have tight clearances like the rudder control system shown here.

most likely will have to be re-placarded to meet a minimum level of functionality. On the other hand, some LSA cockpits are hard to distinguish from larger, more expensive aircraft equipped with glass cockpits, showing the latest in navigational technology (Figure 4-4-2).

The cockpit inspection on these more sophisticated aircraft will be much easier. An inspection of this area should encompass the following areas at a minimum:

- Flight controls
- Instruments
- Seats and seat belts
- Canopy and enclosures

Flight controls. An inspection of the controls in the cockpit should include the area around the rudder pedals as well as the control stick or wheel, for obstructions that may prevent full control deflection, shown in Figure 4-4-3. Loose cables in the cockpit may bind or create abnormal wear if they are allowed to contact the airframe. In Figure 4-4-4 a tight clearance between the rudder cable Nicopress sleeve and the airframe is evident. On LSA in particular, where clearances tend to be small, foreign objects have the potential of fouling the controls to a greater degree than in other aircraft. Slots or gaps in the aircraft structure that are designed to allow full motion of the controls need to be inspected for any objects that may have fallen into them, such as in Figure 4-4-5. Something as small as a pen could restrict control motion.

Instruments. There are two different groups of instruments that can be found in the cockpit: the flight group and the engine group. Depending on the sophistication of the aircraft these may be nothing more than an airspeed indicator, an engine r.p.m. indicator and an oil pressure gauge. More advanced cockpits will have many flight instruments, a pitot static system and engine instruments to monitor temperatures, pressures and speeds for a number of different components. In either case there are some common inspection items that need to be looked at. The instruments are properly marked, all the different lines are secured and will not interfere with the controls.

The instruments indicating range should be clearly marked; caution ranges in yellow and never exceed limits in red. All the range numbers should be legible on all the gauges that have them.

All the instruments should be securely mounted to their panel and any vibration shock mounts should be in working order.

Figure 4-4-5. Inspect slots or gaps in the aircraft structure designed to allow full motion of the controls for foreign objects.

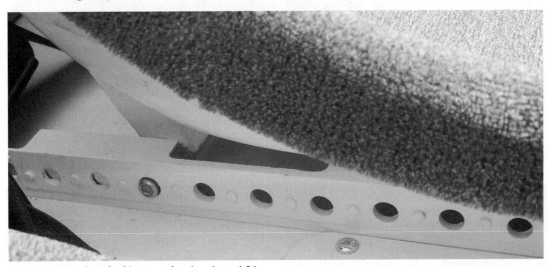

Figure 4-4-6. Seat locking mechanism is an LSA

All the fluid lines to the various instruments should be secured away from any movable controls and not show any evidence of leaks. All electrical wiring should also be secured away from the controls and not hanging down where it can be snagged by a person getting in or out of the cockpit.

Seats and seat belts. The seats in an LSA may be adjustable, similar to standard certificated aircraft, and an inspection should include the seat locking mechanism. See Figure 4-4-6. The locking pin should fully engage and not have a tendency to back out of its locked position in a high vibration environment. These pins should be lubricated to the manufacturer's recommendations to ensure full engagement when actuated. A seat that unexpectedly comes unlocked and slides rearward during takeoff can create a dangerous condition for the pilot by changing the center of gravity of the aircraft. Even worse is the scenario where the pilot tries to pull

him/herself forward by using the control stick and creating a takeoff departure stall situation. The seat supporting structure should also be inspected for cracks and corrosion that may affect the seat's ability to absorb the energy from an impact, or worse allow it to fall apart during a high g maneuver.

Seat belts come in many forms on LSA, but they all have some features in common. They should be designed to keep the occupants in place during high load maneuvers (not the least of which is a parachute deployment) and they should have a metal to metal clasp. A friction clasp is not adequate since these have been shown to slip under both sustained and sudden loads. The webbing in the belts should be inspected for fraying or wear caused by laying over the edge of a member or by a sharp objects in the cockpit and should not be twisted or bunched up. The bolts that connect the belts to the structure should not be worn or grooved and the

Figure 4-4-7. Properly installed seat belt

Figure 4-4-8. Crack radiating from thermometer

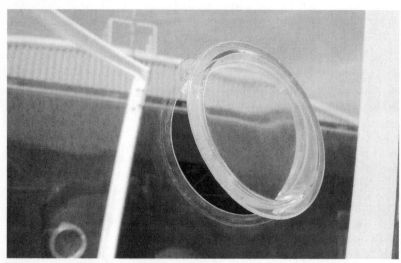

Figure 4-4-9. Built in air vent on a canopy

structure should not be cracked or corroded. See Figure 4-4-7.

Keep in mind that production LSA must demonstrate occupant protection to 9g, or 9 times the weight of the occupant must be restrained by the seatbelt. This should be kept in mind during the inspection.

Canopy and enclosures. The canopy or windshields in an LSA serve a number of functions. They reduce the drag created by the pilot's body, help to streamline that area of the aircraft and protect the pilot from wind, rain, insects and the occasional bird.

The canopy should be carefully inspected for cracks that radiate from stress concentration points, such as the thermometer shown in Figure 4-4-8 or mounting screws that have been overly tightened. Cracks should be stop-drilled immediately to prevent further growth of the crack. Canopies with built-in air vents (Figure 4-4-9) are susceptible to damage from passengers who mistakenly try to open the canopy using the vent hole as a handle. This area should be checked for any imminent cracking.

As an aircraft ages, the acrylic canopy may be subject to crazing. Crazing is the formation of hairline cracks due to stresses that are placed on the material, usually thermal stresses, and they appear as bright streaks in the canopy when the sun strikes them. Figure 4-4-10 shows a canopy that is heavily crazed and well beyond the time when it should be replaced. Crazing will weaken a canopy, so when it is detected, a replacement should be considered.

Section 5
Electrical and Avionics Inspection

The electrical system on an LSA may be as simple as a battery and a starter, as there is no requirement for a radio unless the aircraft is entering certain controlled airspace. Similar to other aspects of LSA, electrical systems will range from ultra simple to complex, with the complex systems coming from kit-built LSA which afford the owner a modern, easy to inspect system. Some of the areas of the system that require inspection are the battery, its box, and associated wiring. The other parts of the system include any wiring and terminal blocks that are used to provide electrical power to other parts of the aircraft.

Battery and box. Traditionally the battery on an aircraft was a lead acid type which required constant maintenance and inspection. Battery technology has advanced over the years and we now have sealed or gel-cell batteries that do not need any servicing. Lead acid batteries require that the electrolyte be replenished with distilled water if the level is below the recommended fill level. This means the battery must be opened from time to time and the level checked. At the same time a condition inspection of the battery should include the specific gravity reading of the electrolyte, which is an indicator of the condition of the cells in the battery. Its electrical capacity, something that will be monitored by the pilot during the starting and in the course of operating the equipment, can also be factored into the condition of the battery. High charge currents after starting or weak starting can indicate a weak battery. This information combined with the date of installation, marked on the top of the battery or in the aircraft records, will help determine if replacement is necessary.

The battery on most LSA will be contained in a battery box, designed to keep hazardous vapors and acid from coming into contact with the airframe and into the cockpit. Because the environment on the inside of the box is hazardous, it should be cleaned with baking soda on a regular basis to remove corrosive deposits, and the vent lines extending to the outside of the airplane should be checked for obstructions and flushed when necessary. After cleaning, the battery and box should be flushed with clean water and a coat of acid-proof paint applied to any area that has been subject to chemical attack. Modern gel-cell batteries are sealed and do not vent corrosive gases, so maintenance will be less if a gel-cell has been installed. Inspection of the battery box area should include checking for the following:

- The battery is secured in the box and will not come loose in negative g maneuvers.

- The box is secured and positive leads leaving the box are in no danger of shorting with the airframe.

- Vent lines are clear and functional.

- Corrosion has not occurred on the airframe in the vicinity of the box.

Terminal blocks. Terminal blocks should be inspected for any wires that are loose from the screw connections or posts. The crimped ends or terminations should also be checked to make sure that no wires are coming out of the connection or that no strands are broken. Figure 4-5-1 shows a terminal block that is mounted externally, and is also indicative of one of new challenges presented by ELSA aircraft. Normally, an aircraft would not be

Figure 4-4-10. Severe crazing on a canopy which must be replaced.

designed with an exposed voltage regulator, master switch relay and the terminal buss. But if the owner intends to fly only on dry days, this system should work fine. The inspector should pay careful attention to aerodynamic loads that may loosen wires and connections in a case like this, and any damage that may occur due to exposure to the elements or impacts by foreign objects.

Some excellent wiring standards are contained in the FAA Advisory Circular 43.13. Among those are:

- Wires and cables should be supported by suitable clamps, grommets or other devices at intervals of not more than 24 inches, except when contained in troughs, ducts or conduits.

- Wires and cables should be supported to prevent excessive movement in areas of high vibration.

Figure 4-5-1. Externally mounted terminal block

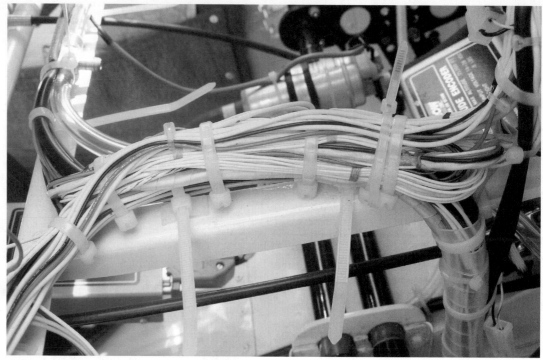

Figure 4-5-2. Example of proper wire routing and security

Figure 4-6-1. Inspect control surface bearings with removable hardware for binding or misalignment.

- Grommets, plastic liners or phenolic blocks should be installed in holes that wire passes through to prevent chafing on the airframe or other components of the aircraft.

- Minimum bend radii of wire groups or bundles should not be less than 10 times the outside diameter of the largest wire or cable, except at terminal strips or in a reversal within a bundle where the radius can be 3 times the diameter.

- Wires should not come closer than 1/2 inch

to mechanical control cables when light pressure is applied to the wire or control cables. Support must be added if this occurs.

- Wires should be replaced if they have been crushed or kinked.

- Plastic terminal lugs showing evidence of breaks, cracks, dirt or moisture should be replaced.

- Terminal strips should not show signs of heat damage or physical damage.

For more in-depth information on wiring, AC 43-13 has one entire section that is dedicated to wiring and installation of electrical systems.

As an example of proper wire routing and security, Figure 4-5-2 shows several wire bundles behind the instrument panel of an LSA with tie wraps that are used at regular intervals to provide support. A slight pressure on the wire bundles should not move the bundle and cause chafing or interference with the control cables.

The connections made to all radios behind the instrument panel should be inspected to reveal any problems that may result in binding of the control cables, or failure of a particular piece of equipment. Avionics, gauges and indicators should pass a functional check during the inspection, and this may in turn reveal problems with other parts of the electrical system. With the engine running, all electrical systems should be turned on to create a full load situation for the alternator. The radios should operate normally, with no abnormal noises in the audio system, and lights should not flicker, indicating a fluctuating voltage.

Circuit breaker connections should be checked, and the condition of the breakers should also be inspected, including signs of heat damage.

Section 6

Rigging and Assembly

The inspection of the rigging of any aircraft is an opportunity to correct any small handling problems that have occurred during flight. Perhaps the aircraft is slightly wing heavy, or is not cruising at the best possible speed. This is the time to correct those problems and also the time to make sure that everything is adjusted to where the manufacturer first meant it to be. This is also the time to inspect an aircraft that is frequently assembled and disassembled to check the components which are cycled in and out of fittings on the airframe. This includes pins, bolts, locking or castellated nuts, and other fastening features used to properly configure structural elements, control systems and fuel systems. The annual condition inspection should include a disassembly and reassembly operation of airplane to ensure all component work as intended and have not worn beyond limits recommended by the manufacturer. Some common wear items are:

Figure 4-6-2. Main structural attachment pins

- Control surface bearings that have removable hardware (Figure 4-6-1) should be inspected for binding or misalignment caused by improper assembly.

- Main structural attachment pins (Figure 4-6-2) should be visually inspected for steps or signs of wear that would result in freeplay in the joint.

- Control linkages should be inspected for dents or bends from abuse during the assembly/disassembly process.

- Quick-disconnect fuel lines should be inspected for evidence of leaking and stress that may result in a fluid joint or tubing failure.

Chapter 5

PROPULSION
system inspection

Section 1

Engine Theory

In the early days of aviation, many internal combustion engine designs were attempted as inventors sought the ideal solution to powered flight. The Wright brothers settled on their own in-line, four-cylinder design after realizing there were no manufacturers capable of meeting their power (9 hp.), weight and low vibration requirements. Their 1903 Flyer engine, built by Charles Taylor, produced 16 hp., and the recent Centennial of Flight Celebration resulted in a Flyer engine capable of 20 hp., still giving a relatively high weight/power ratio of 10 lbs/hp. Figure 5-1-1 (next page) shows the Centennial reproduction engine in action. Simultaneous to the work of the Wrights, Charles Manly was developing a radial engine that would power the Aerodrome designed by Samuel Langley of the Smithsonian. This aircraft was twice launched unsuccessfully from a houseboat on the Potomac River in 1903, and while the aircraft's wings twisted under aerodynamic loads, Manly's engine was delivering up to 52 hp., a weight/power ratio of 4 lbs/hp. This engine, shown in Figure 5-1-2 (next page) was truly remarkable for its time.

The ignition systems used on engines at the turn of the century varied from hot tubes (essentially large glow plugs) to flame ignition, to high and low-tension magneto spark ignition systems. The Wrights chose to use a low-tension magneto system consisting of a set of points located inside the cylinder that would spark as they opened. Glenn Curtiss, on the other hand, used what we would consider a more conventional type of spark ignition: the high-tension magneto and spark plugs.

Learning Objectives:

- *Engine Theory*
- *The Engine Condition Inspection*
- *The Engine Electrical System*
- *The Intake System*
- *The Exhaust System*
- *Engine Cooling*
- *Lubrication Systems*
- *Fuel System Inspection*
- *Gearbox/ Reduction Drive System*
- *Propellers*
- *Engine Mount and Controls*

Left: **An engine that is completely exposed is easier to inspect and service.**

Figure 5-1-1. Centennial reproduction engine

As aviation became more refined prior to World War I, both two-stroke and four-stroke power-plants were seen on aircraft. Engines came in rotary (the block and cylinders revolve around a fixed crankshaft), radial (the crankshaft rotates instead of the cylinders), and in-line styles with a wide range of displacements and numbers of cylinders. Several two-stroke engines from England and the U.S. appeared on aircraft, providing in the neighborhood of 3 lbs/hp. Since a two-stroke engine develops power on every stroke of the piston, these engines were generally lighter than their four-stroke counterparts. Reliability of the two-stroke engines was less, however, and four-stroke engines became the dominant choice for aircraft powerplants up until recently.

With the advent of powered hang gliders in the early 1980's, two-stroke engines have once again become viable choices to power aircraft. Low weight/power ratios of around 1 lb/hp for modern two-stroke engines make these power-plants ideal for smaller airframes. The inclusion of many two-place ultralights as LSA brings two-stroke technology into the LSA inspection program.

Two Stroke Cycle Engines

The operation of a two-stroke cycle, or two-cycle engine is fundamentally different than the more common four-stroke cycle engine found on most cars and larger production aircraft. Figure 5-1-3 shows the cross-section of a two-stroke engine operating over a complete cycle. Most of these engines do not have valves in the head as is common in a four-cycle engine. Instead, the mixture (air plus gasoline mixed with oil at an approximately 50:1 ratio) is sucked into the bottom end of the engine during the *compression stroke* of the piston. Some Rotax two-cycle engines (models 447 and 503) have ports in the sides of the cylinder which open as the piston travels up, drawing the mixture into the

Figure 5-1-2. Manly's engine

Photo courtesy of Smithsonian Institution

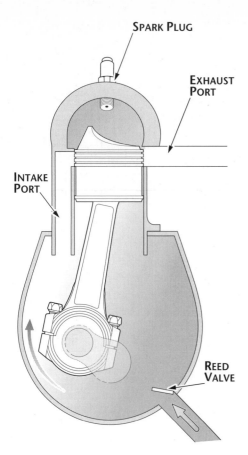

SPARK PLUG

EXHAUST PORT

INTAKE PORT

REED VALVE

INTAKE/ COMPRESSION STROKE

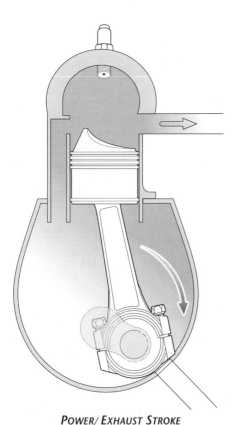

POWER/ EXHAUST STROKE

Figure 5-1-3. Cross-section of a two-stroke engine in operation

engine under the slight vacuum caused by the upstroke. The Rotax 582 series engines have a rotary valve on the crankcase that regulates the combustible mixture into the engine during the compression stroke, shown in Figure 5-1-4.

When the piston is within a few degrees of the top of its stroke, or top dead center (TDC), the spark plug is fired and ignition occurs. The rotational position of the crankshaft at ignition is usually 10 to 20° before top dead center (BTDC), as specified by the manufacturer. This amount of advance is less than what is found on four-stroke engines due to the fact that a gas/oil mix will burn faster than gasoline alone. The addition of oil in the fuel of a two-stroke engine provides lubrication to the bottom end of the engine, but it also reduces the octane rating of the fuel resulting in quicker combustion.

After combustion, the piston is pushed downward driving the crankshaft in the *power stroke.* As the piston travels downward, it passes by a port in the cylinder that is connected to the exhaust manifold. The excess pressure in the cylinder is relieved when the port is opened, venting the exhaust to the muffler. Shortly after the exhaust is vented, another port is exposed as the piston moves downward, allowing the mixture in the crankcase to be forced into the cylinder under the slight positive pressure created by the piston movement. When the piston begins traveling upward, it closes off all open ports and the mixture is compressed for combustion, starting the process all over again.

Figure 5-1-4. Rotary valve on the crankcase of a Rotax 582 series engine
Courtesy of Solo Avation

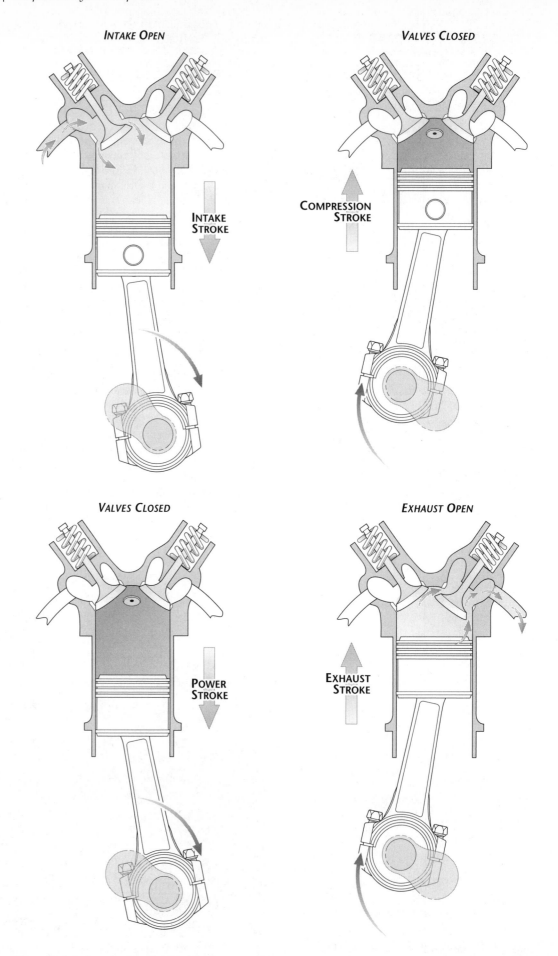

Figure 5-1-5. Four-stroke cycle engine

Figure 5-1-6. A typical valve train.

Two-stroke engines not only gain power by operating at higher speeds than four stroke engines, but they develop power on every downstroke of the piston. Four-stroke cycle engines require a non-power producing cycle to complete the combustion process. The speed advantage of a two-stroke engine is due to the lack of moving parts, mainly the camshaft and valve train which are not needed in a two-stroke but are found in four-stroke engines.

Four Stroke Cycle Engines

In a four-stroke cycle engine, diagrammed in Figure 5-1-5, the piston must move up and down twice for every power producing stroke. The first stroke is the intake stroke, where the piston moves downward creating a slight vacuum in the cylinder which draws the air/fuel mixture into the combustion chamber. The intake valve is open and the exhaust valve is closed. On the next upward stroke, both the intake and exhaust valves are closed and the mixture is compressed. As in the case of the two-stroke engine, the spark plug is fired before the piston reaches the top of its travel, giving the mixture time to complete its burn while the piston is force downward from the expanding charge, driving the crankshaft. The last stroke is the exhaust stroke, where the piston travels upward again, but this time with the exhaust valve open to vent the combustion gases.

The entry and exit of gases to and from the combustion chamber (cylinder volume above the piston) is accomplished through valves that open and close under actuation by a camshaft. The cam is typically located in the bottom end of the engine and is driven by the crankshaft through a 1:2 gear reduction drive. This is a simpler design than what is found in most modern automobile engines that use an overhead cam design, where the cam is driven by a belt or chain. A tappet body rides on the camshaft and translates the rotary motion into an up and down motion which is transmitted to the pushrod. The pushrod extends from the engine block to the top of the cylinder and actuates the rocking motion of the rocker arms, and they in turn push the valves up and down. A typical valve train is shown in Figure 5-1-6.

Intake and exhaust valves have not changed much over the years in terms of their shape and function. Early valves were either one-piece cast iron or a two-piece assembly, where a tool steel stem was riveted to a cast iron head. The early exhaust valves were frequently the reason for engine failure because of the high tem-

Figure 5-1-7. A valve broken off at the valve stem and embedded in the top of the piston from a 1925 Thomas Morse MB-3.

peratures they are exposed to, on the order of 1,400° F. Figure 5-1-7 shows a valve that failed in a 1925 Thomas Morse MB-3, broken off at the valve stem and embedded in the top of the piston. Modern exhaust valves are designed to withstand these high temperatures to the recommended overhaul time of the engine, sometimes thousands of hours.

The valve train found on a four stroke engine adds a degree of complexity and weight not found on a two stroke engine. The inspection will take this into account.

Section 2

The Engine Condition Inspection

Historically associated with aircraft, the four-stroke air cooled engine has been employed in the aviation community dating back to the early rotary engines of World War I. These engines have more moving parts than two-cycle engines and a larger weight to power ratio, but are cleaner burning and tend to be more reliable than two cycles. Common manufacturers of these engines include Textron Lycoming, Teledyne Continental, Jabiru, Rotax and HKS. Examples are shown in Figure 5-2-1.

Air-cooled two-stroke cycle aircraft engines include those manufactured by Hirth and Rotax, with an example shown in Figure 5-2-2. As previously mentioned, the use of two-stroke engines has increased since the advent of powered hang gliders, with weight/power ratios of up to 1 lb/hp.

The Borescope

Before detailed engine inspection procedures are covered, one of the most valuable inspection tools will be described here: the borescope. The borescope is an invaluable tool to obtain an up-close examination of cylinders, pistons, valves, and other engine components not easily accessed without disassembly of parts of the engine. Figure 5-2-3 shows a typical borescope, designed to fit into small openings such as the spark plug hole to obtain a view inside the engine cylinder. A borescope should be considered a mandatory diagnostic tool for the cylinder if a compression check indicates that there is excessive leakage. The cylinder walls can be inspected for scoring, the top of the piston can be inspected for burn-through, and the valves can be inspected for damage and improper seating.

A properly sized borescope should pass into the cylinder through the spark plug hole, and be capable of articulating so that a view upward, at the valves, can be obtained. The valves, valve seating area, cylinder walls, and top of the piston can be examined for abnormal wear which will be discussed below.

The borescope can be found in a couple of different forms, a rigid tube outfitted with mirrors and prisms and a light source or as a bundle of optic fibers that has an eye piece and is flexible. The bundle of fibers can be made to articulate with the use of a manual control. Some of the more sophisticated models can be connected to cameras, video and computers for specific inspections. A simpler form will be sufficient for any two or four cycle engine inspection.

Overall Condition

The beginning of any inspection is the gathering of the checklist, the manufacturer's manuals as well as the maintenance records for the engine. A few minutes spent reviewing the paperwork can save many hours of wasted time in the future.

Before any engine can be inspected it must be viewed as a whole and then the individual sections need to be considered. An overall look at the engine can reveal multiple problems such as oil leaks, broken wires, exhaust leaks, coolant leaks, cracked baffles and loose safeties.

Figure 5-2-1. Four-stroke air cooled engines

They are just a few of the things that can be seen without having to disassemble much of the engine. The second thing that must be done is a thorough cleaning of the engine to remove any dirt and oil.

The overall condition inspection of an air cooled engine block should reveal no oily stains that would indicate faulty seals, loose fasteners or cracked components such as the engine block. Typical signs of tired seals are shown in Figure 5-2-4. On two-stroke engines, the front crankshaft bearing seal (fan-side) and the rear crankshaft seal (power take off, or PTO side) should be inspected for leakage. It may be difficult to gain direct access to these seals in an inspection because of pulleys, accessories and the output gear box blocking a direct view. Covers and inspection plugs should be removed to at least gain a view of the surrounding seal area, to inspect for the *evidence* of seal failure indicated by oil streaking, staining or dirt accumulation caused by oily residue on the engine.

In the case of the Rotax geared engines, failure of the rear seal can be detected by oil that has been slung out by the flywheel and through

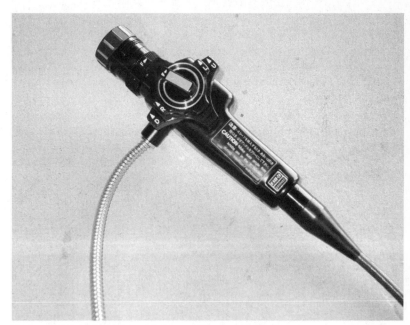

Figure 5-2-3. Typical borescope used for inspecting

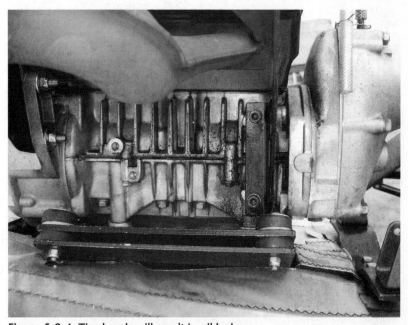

Figure 5-2-4. Tired seals will result in oil leaks.

Figure 5-2-2. Rotax air-cooled two-stroke cycle aircraft engines

Figure 5-2-5. Failure of the rear seal indicated by an oily residue near the gear box vent hole.

Figure 5-2-6. Abnormal rust in the crankcase

the vent hole between the gear box and the engine. An oily residue on the side of the engine will generally be oriented downwind from the vent hole, and may appear as a slight discoloration as seen in Figure 5-2-5. Seal failure can lead to bearing failure, and so replacement of leaky seals is highly recommended before more expensive repairs result.

The vibration levels on internal combustion engines can be high, especially on two-stroke engines, and for this reason cover plates and bolted joints should be checked for flexibility and looseness. Fasteners may require a periodic retorque. Engine manufacturers typically publish recommended intervals for retorqueing fasteners, and these guidelines should be observed during the inspection. Cylinder head nuts and exhaust manifold screws are the more common fasteners to loosen over time.

Many two-cycle designs are unique in that the bottom end of the engine (crankshaft and connecting rods) can frequently be inspected by simply removing the intake hardware and the manifold. Using a borescope, the crankshaft should be carefully inspected for signs of abnormal wear or rust. Again, unlike four-cycle engines, the crankcase has a direct path to the outside environment through the intake manifold or exhaust manifold, depending on where the engine stopped when it was shut down. This direct path will allow moisture to enter and condense on steel parts, causing rust to form as shown in Figure 5-2-6. During periods of inactivity, two-cycle engines should be plugged on the exhaust end, and a bag should be tied on the intake over the air cleaner to prevent moisture from entering the engine.

The top-end of the engine consisting of the cylinders and heads should be inspected for damaged fins and debris that may be lodged in the cooling fins, causing a reduction in cooling capacity. The inspection of the exterior of the

Figure 5-2-7. Cracked fin in a cylinder

cylinder should include a careful examination for cracks that appear at the base of the fins; difficult to detect but critical for safety of flight. Figure 5-2-7 shows a cracked fin.

Overheated heads are more prone to cracking, and the inspector should consider the operational history to determine if such an event happened. Cracks at the base of the fin require the part to be rejected as they can propagate through the entire structure. Fins may also be bent or dented, and these can be left alone as long as there is adequate airflow around them and they are not the source of any cracks. Fins that are broken can be filed to remove rough, jagged shapes as long as they are not located around features such as the spark plug hole. Heat dissipation is more critical around the spark plug hole and other features where thermal expansion and contraction can result in large stress concentrations, potentially causing cracks to form. For this reason, if fins are broken around geometrical features it is recommended that the affected part be rejected.

The cylinder head of an air cooled engine is usually a separate part that is threaded or bolted on to the top of the cylinder, and leakage can occur at the head/cylinder interface because of the high pressures in the combustion chamber. This area should be inspected for any evidence of exhaust leakage that is not part of the exhaust system.

The cylinders are bolted to the crankcase and also experience high stress and vibration levels that can result in leakage occurring around the cylinder base gasket. Evidence of this may be found in the accumulation of dirt on top of an oily residue, as seen in Figure 5-2-8. Some slight leakage of this nature is acceptable if it does not result in the formation of oil drops on the bottom of the engine, but it should be monitored for increased leakage.

Removing the exhaust manifold will reveal the amount of carbon build-up on the inside of the engine. For two-stroke engines, normal, acceptable carbon build-up is less than 0.020 in. thick (0.5 mm), uniformly distributed on the sides of the exhaust area as well as on the top inside area of the cylinder. Figure 5-2-9 shows approximately 0.020 inches of carbon build-up on a two-stroke exhaust port. Thicker layers of carbon require the engine to be decarbonized to achieve its rated power.

Again, an advantage of the two stroke design is that much of the interior of the engine is exposed for inspection. The piston can be examined on both the intake and exhaust sides for scoring that may have occurred due to the presence of foreign particles, as shown in Figure 5-2-10. A small amount of scoring *above* the piston rings is acceptable, but the area below the rings the

Figure 5-2-8. Accumulation of dirt on top of an oily residue indicates leakage occurring around the cylinder base gasket.

Figure 5-2-9. Carbon build-up on the exhaust port of a two-stroke engine

Figure 5-2-10. Vertical scoring that has occurred due to the presence of foreign particles.

Figure 5-2-11. Combustion gas blow-by past the rings indicated by staining extending below the ring area.

Figure 5-2-12. A hole burned through the top of a piston.

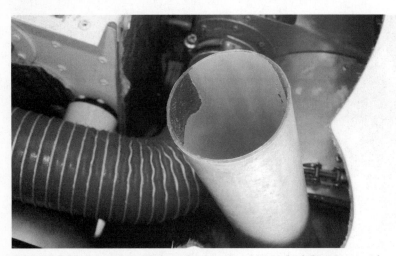

Figure 5-2-13. Properly tuned engine burning 100 LL fuel showing residue deposits on the inside of the exhaust pipe.

piston should be smooth. Blow-by of combustion gases past the rings will be revealed by a staining that extends below the ring area, seen in Figure 5-2-11. This indicates that the rings are failing or stuck and should be replaced. Ring wear is evaluated with the pistons removed and is measured by measuring the end gap in the ring with a feeler gauge and comparing the measured value to acceptable limits published by the manufacturer. The lands (ridges) between the piston ring grooves should be inspected for breakage and wear that exceeds the manufacturer's recommended clearance. The clearance between the ring and groove can be checked with a feeler gauge. Excessive clearance requires that the piston and rings be replaced.

The top of the piston should appear smooth with no irregular marks or indentations that would indicate foreign particle damage or hot spots, leading to a burn-through. Like the intake and top cylinder areas, the piston dome on two-stroke engines should have no more than 0.02 in. thick build-up of carbon; more would require a decarbonizing process.

In the event of overspeeding the engine, many manufacturers will have a required inspection to determine if damage occurred. Rotax, for instance, recommends that the cylinders of the engine be removed and the pistons inspected for seizure. Likewise if the cylinder head temperature limits were exceeded, the cylinders should be removed and the pistons inspected for seizure and depressions in the piston crown.

Damage from high temperature operation is serious, sometimes resulting in catastrophic engine failure. The causes of a high temperature event can be improper cooling, an overly lean mixture, fuel with the wrong octane rating, or faulty ignition timing, all of which can cause pre-ignition or detonation. These conditions can be so severe that a hole is burned through the top of the piston as shown in Figure 5-2-12. Any abnormal engine behavior after cylinder head temperatures have been elevated should be regarded as a warning of possible high temperature engine damage.

On the other end of the spectrum is shock cooling. Liquid-cooled Rotax engines are designed with very tight clearances between the piston and cylinder, and because of this they cannot tolerate large fluctuations in temperature that result in excessive thermal expansion and contraction. An engine that is shut down while flying on a cold day, and then restarted has the potential to send cold water (from the radiator) into a hot engine, resulting in a sudden contraction of the cylinder that seizes the piston. If there is any suspicion that this occurred, an inspection should focus on the piston and cylinder walls for evidence of scoring. If found, an engine teardown would follow.

On four-stroke engines, the removal of the exhaust and intake manifolds is optional during the inspection. The examination of the color of the residue left on the exhaust stack and an examination of the spark plugs is usually an adequate indicator of residues deposited inside the cylinder. Figure 5-2-13 shows a residue deposited on the inside of the exhaust pipe in an engine that is properly tuned and burning 100 LL fuel. A light brown color is an indication of a proper mixture and combustion temperature, with no abnormalities such as excessive oil consumption in the operation.

The condition of the cylinder walls, tops of the pistons and the valve faces can be inspected with the use of a borescope. The borescope is inserted through the spark plug hole and the condition of the cylinder walls should be inspected for scoring (vertical scratches) caused by stuck rings, or overall wear on the cylinder walls indicated by a horizontal step in the surface at the top of the piston stroke. The amount of rust on plain steel cylinder liners on an engine that has not been run for a period of time can also be seen and evaluated. This can lead to accelerated wear of other parts of the cylinder because rust is harder than steel. One-time events where small amounts of rust (less than 1% of the cylinder surface area) are detected will not require servicing, but cylinder reconditioning should be performed if the rusting is more extensive. Other cylinder wall defects caused by servicing include improper cross hatching during the honing process, or wear that has removed a plating layer as part of the reconditioning process.

Valve Train Inspection - Four Stroke Cycle Engines

The valve train on an air cooled engine should be carefully examined during the inspection. The following items can be inspected by removing the rocker box covers on the cylinders to expose the top end of the valve train (Figure 5-2-14):

- Metal particles in the rocker box are indications of excessive wear or partial failure of the valve mechanism.

- Excessive side clearance or galling of the rocker arm side should be corrected with shims or other recommendations by the manufacturer.

- Cracked, broken or chipped rocker arms, valve springs or spring retainers.

- Excessive valve stem clearance. Use the manufacturer's recommended procedure for determining acceptable play in the valve stem.

- Evidence of insufficient lubrication. A dry

Figure 5-2-14. Valve train on an air cooled engine can be carefully examined by removing the rocker box covers.

rocker arm can indicate that the oil passage in the push rod is plugged.

- Too much oil in the rocker box. This may be caused by a plugged drain.

- Excessive sludge in the rocker box. This can be caused by excessive temperature of the rocker box, which in turn may be caused by improper cooling.

- Variation in valve clearance not explained by normal wear. This could be caused by a bent push rod or other component that has worn abnormally beyond acceptable limits.

Valve clearances should be verified during the inspection as being within normal limits. An exhaust valve that does not seat entirely will allow hot gases to escape and cause the valve to warp or fail. Intake valves not seating properly can cause backfiring. A visual and tactile inspection of the valves will usually confirm normal seating, but the cylinder compression check discussed below will definitively determine if the valves are not functioning properly.

Engine Compression Check

Prior to the compression check there are certain safety procedures that must be observed:

- The ignition must be off

- All the sparkplug leads should be disconnected

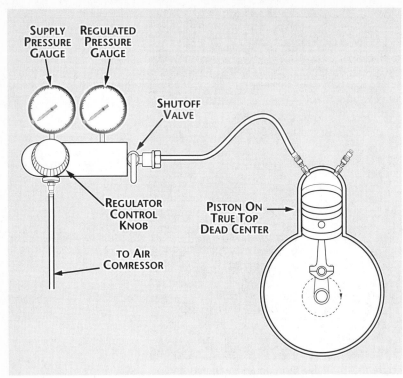

Figure 5-2-15. Compression tester

- Burned or warped valves
- Carbon particles between the face and the seat of the valve or valves
- Early or late valve timing

Compression checks are usually performed on a hot engine so that the valves and rings are freshly lubricated and all the metals are at their operational temperatures and expansion rates. A differential compression tester is the most common tool for evaluating engine compression by pressurizing the engine cylinder through a restricting orifice that creates a pressure drop based on air flow rate. A typical compression tester design is shown in Figure 5-2-15. The shop air line is connected to the tester unit containing the orifice with a pressure gauge mounted on the upstream side of the orifice. Downstream of the orifice is another pressure gauge and air line connected to the cylinder usually through the spark plug hole of the cylinder. A measure of air flow rate is obtained by observing the differential pressures on the gauges. Air flow through the system can only occur around the valves and rings, and so the larger the pressure drop, the more likely the valves or rings are not functioning properly.

Differential compression tester. The differential pressure tester is designed to check the compression of aircraft engines by measuring the leakage through the cylinders caused by worn or damaged components. Operation of the compression tester is based on the principle that, for any given airflow through a fixed orifice, a constant pressure drop across that orifice will result. The restrictor orifice dimensions in the differential pressure tester should be sized for the particular engine as follows:

- Engines up to 1,000 cubic inch displacement: 0.040-inch orifice diameter, 0.250 inch long, 60° approach angle.
- Engines in excess of 1,000 cubic inch displacement: 0.060-inch orifice diameter, 0.250 inch long, 60° approach angle.

The differential pressure tester requires the application of air pressure to the cylinder being tested with the piston at top-center compression stroke.

To ensure accuracy, the differential compression tester must be tested using a *master orifice*. The master orifice is a calibration standard that establishes the acceptable cylinder pressure leakage limit for the test equipment being used and the atmospheric conditions at the time of the test. Some newer model compression testers have a master orifice built in.

- The area of the prop arc should be clear
- The fuel selector is switched off
- Always stand clear of the propeller arc when the cylinders are being pressurized

There are specific steps to be followed in analyzing the effectiveness of the compression stroke in the engine. The power developed from the engine is only as good as its ability to contain the compressed and expanding gases in the cylinder. This is why compression is checked as a health monitoring activity. As a starting point, the engine should be turned over a few times by hand (usually through the prop with ignition "off") to evaluate the engine's compression-induced resistance. Near-uniform compression should be felt on all cylinders as the prop is rotated. Variations in compression at this stage can be due to valve or piston ring failure, or if the variation is small, they may simply be caused by the difference in oil that is helping the rings seal the piston. If little resistance is felt while pulling the propeller through a compression stroke, a cylinder can be suspected of having a serious valve or piston ring problem.

Lack of cylinder compression can usually be attributed to one or more of the following conditions:

- Incorrect valve clearances
- Worn, scuffed or damaged pistons
- Excessive wear of piston rings and cylinder walls

As with other maintenance operations, the recommendations of the engine manufacturer must be followed closely. Specific instructions regarding compression testing and evaluating the test results may be found in Service Bulletins or other publications issued by the manufacturer.

General guidelines for performing a differential compression test are:

1. Perform the compression test as soon as possible after engine shutdown to provide uniform lubrication of cylinder walls and rings.

2. Remove the most accessible spark plug from the cylinder or cylinders and install a spark plug adapter in the spark plug hole.

3. Connect the compression tester assembly to a 100- to 150-p.s.i. compressed air supply. With the shutoff valve on the compression tester closed, adjust the regulator of the compression tester to obtain 80 p.s.i. on the regulated pressure gauge

4. Hand tighten the test adapter in the spark plug hole, with O-ring into the cylinder

5. Place a thumb over the end of the adapter and rotate the prop until the piston's compression blows against your thumb. This will place the piston in the compression stroke, near TDC.

6. Connect a hose from the adapter in the cylinder under test to the tester via a quick connect fitting.

7. Slowly open the fill valve approximately 1/8 turn while holding the propeller, until moderate resistance is felt at the prop. Carefully rotate the prop back and forth through TDC until a positive detent is felt. Hold the prop at TDC to minimize the tendency for rotation.

CAUTION: *Cylinder pressure will slowly rise to 80 p.s.i. and prop may rotate. Use extreme caution.*

8. Open the fill valve completely while maintaining a strong grip on the propeller.

9. If necessary, readjust the regulator to 80 p.s.i.

10. Read the relative pressure in the cylinder under test, on the cylinder gauge.

11. Record the results as a differential reading:

xx p.s.i.
80 p.s.i.

If low compression is obtained on any cylinder, turn the engine through with the starter or re-start and run the engine to takeoff power and re-check the cylinder or cylinders having low compression. If the low compression is not corrected, remove the rocker-box cover (on 4-stroke engines) and check the valve clearance to determine if the difficulty is caused by inadequate valve clearance. If the low compression is not caused by inadequate valve clearance, place a fiber drift on the rocker arm immediately over the valve stem and tap the drift several times with a 1- to 2-pound hammer to dislodge any foreign material that may be lodged between the valve and valve seat. After staking the valve in this manner, rotate the engine with the starter and re-check the compression. Do not make a compression check after staking a valve until the crankshaft has been rotated either with the starter or by hand to re-seat the valve in the normal manner. The higher seating velocity obtained when staking the valve will indicate valve seating even though valve seats are slightly eccentric.

Cylinders having compression below the minimum specified after staking should be further checked to determine whether leakage is past the exhaust valve, intake valve or piston. Excessive leakage can be detected:

- At the exhaust valve by listening for air leakage at the exhaust outlet

- At the intake valve by escaping air at the air intake

- Past the piston rings by escaping air at the engine breather outlets

The wheeze test is another method of detecting leaking intake and exhaust valves. In this test, as the piston is moved to TDC on the compression stroke, the faulty valve may be detected by listening for a wheezing sound in the exhaust outlet or intake duct.

Next to valve blow-by, the most frequent cause of compression leakage is excessive leakage past the piston. This leakage may occur because of lack of oil. To check this possibility, squirt engine oil into the cylinder and around the piston. Then re-check the compression. If this procedure raises compression to or above the minimum required, continue to use the cylinder in service. If the cylinder pressure readings still do not meet the minimum requirement, replace the cylinder and rings. When it is necessary to replace a cylinder as a result of low compression, record the cylinder number and the compression value of the newly installed cylinder on the compression check sheet.

Be advised that on geared engines, performing a differential compression test may not be possible due to the high torque values created at the prop during cylinder pressurization. In fact, this could be a dangerous operation as the prop may be impossible to stop when 80 p.s.i. air is admitted to the cylinder. Furthermore, finding top dead center on the engine will be difficult because the engine turns faster than the prop. Two alternative methods are suggested:

- Use a source air pressure that is lower than 80 p.s.i., perhaps 30 p.s.i., so that the prop can be safely restrained during pressurization.

- Use an automotive-type compression tester, which relies on dynamic compression by turning the engine over while measuring the compression. A standard method can be adopted so that the results can be compared from check to check.

Section 3

The Engine Electrical System

Many LSA only have a basic electrical system that recharges the small battery used for starting and an ignition system. More sophisticated LSA will have a system that can handle various communication and navigation devices as well.

Figure 5-3-1. Self-contained aircraft magneto

Figure 5-3-2. Block-mounted magneto system *Photo courtesy of SoLo Aviation*

The Ignition System

Internal combustion engines have an electrical ignition system that provides the spark which ignites the mixture. Aircraft engines usually have one of three types of ignition systems:

- Magneto with breaker points
- Coil with breaker points
- Capacitive Discharge Ignition (CDI), no breaker points

The first type, the magneto powered ignition system, is most commonly found on general aviation aircraft that have adopted the magneto as a standard of reliability dating back to the earliest days of aviation. The Wright 1908 and 1909 machines used a magneto system similar in operation to the unison magnetos found on new production aircraft today.

A basic magneto generates a pulse of energy through the rotation of an armature in a magnetic field. This energy is stored in the coil windings until the points open causing the magnetic field to collapse. This collapse generates a high voltage pulse which is directed to the spark plug at the advanced firing position of the cylinder. The advantage of magneto ignition is that an external power source is not needed; the magneto generates the spark independent of the aircraft's electrical system. Figure 5-3-1 shows a self-contained aircraft magneto.

The second type of ignition system is commonly found on automobiles, and has been part of the automotive industry for the last forty years. A coil is energized by the vehicle's electrical system, and at the right moment a set of contact points are opened causing a spark to occur. The coil ignition system is dependent on the vehicle's electrical system, so if the alternator fails and the battery discharges, the engine may stop running. For this reason, this type of ignition system is rarely found on aircraft.

The third type of system has recently become more popular because of its reliability and lack of moving parts. The capacitive discharge ignition system, or CDI, stores energy in large capacitors as opposed to coils which are used in the first two systems. A reluctance transducer detects the proper crankshaft angle when ignition will occur. The reluctance transducer can sense the passing of a piece of ferrous metal which is attached to the crankshaft, giving the engine its timing information for ignition to occur. Like the magneto system, a generator integral to the engine system provides the power.

Inspection of the Ignition System

Magneto system. It is necessary to inspect the points and set the timing for the magneto system during the inspection since normal part wear will change the ignition timing. Engines with self-contained magnetos that are attached as an accessory to the motor have the advantage that the whole unit can be rotated to change ignition timing. This can save considerable time over a system that has points fixed to the engine block which must be accessed through a small hole (usually in the flywheel). Figure 5-3-2 shows a block-mounted magneto system. For the latter system, the timing process involves setting the points to open at the manufacturer's specified crank position, and then checking the opening gap using a feeler gauge. The process can be iterative, since adjusting the points to obtain the proper opening gap will affect the opening time.

The use of a timing device that detects the exact moment when the points open is a necessary tool to time a magneto-equipped engine. Shown in Figure 5-3-3, these devices emit an audible tone or illuminate a light indicating that the points have opened. Since nearly all aircraft engines have redundant ignition systems, the advantage of a timing indicator is that it tells the operator when both points have been properly timed. In addition to detecting the opening of the points, an accurate measure of the crank angle must be obtained. Some engines have a mark on the flywheel which will point to a mark on the block at the exact time that the points should open. This can greatly aid in the timing process. In the absence of a mark, other devices are available that will find the exact crank position by detecting the position of the piston in the number one cylinder.

Timing of self contained magnetos by changing their orientation is not the complete process in their adjustment. The points inside of a self contained magneto must also be set relative to the pole of the rotor magnet (called *E* gap), and the gap of the breaker points must also be set. These adjustments are usually not necessary during the annual inspection, but should be considered if the magneto is not producing an adequate spark.

CDI system. The CDI system works by setting two reference bars on the engine flywheel so that they are at a certain distance and rotational position to the transducer pick-ups located on the edge of the flywheel. See Figure 5-3-4. The engine crankshaft is oriented per the manufacturer's specification while the bars are set up using feeler gauges. Since the bars are located on the flywheel, the whole process is simplified since the exact crankshaft angle is defined during the set-up. Two generator coils inside of the flywheel are dedicated to powering the ignition system, and the other engine coils function to power the aircraft electrical system. These coils

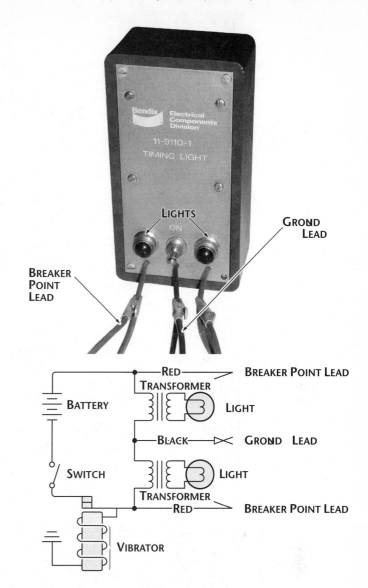

Figure 5-3-3. Timing device for a magneto-equipped engine

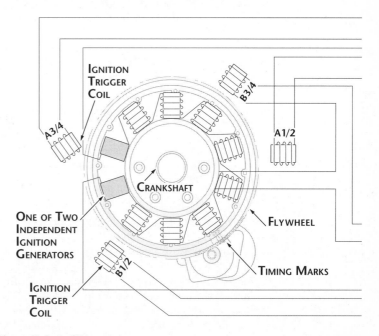

Figure 5-3-4. CDI system

Figure 5-3-5. Plug connectors

Figure 5-3-6. Two types of plugs found in LSA engines; non-shielded design and shielded design

charge capacitors which are discharged to the ignition coils for plug firing when the transducers are triggered.

Inspection of the CDI system is minimal, since there are few moving parts to wear out. The integrity of all wiring should be inspected, and evidence of burn through, breaks, or wear should be noted.

Plug Wires and Connectors

The high tension leads passing from the coil or CDI boxes to the spark plugs should be inspected for proper routing and condition. Since these leads carry a very high voltage, any breaks or discontinuities in the leads will affect the spark at the plug. Exposure of the leads to moisture in the event of flight into precipitation

should be minimized by routing wires away from engine cowl cooling vents. Heavy oil deposits on ignition leads can also cause shorting to occur.

The plug connectors (Figure 5-3-5) should be checked for cracks, burn-off, dampness and fouling. The plug boot on the end of the connector should be intact to shield the system from moisture.

Plug caps need to be matched to the spark plug in two ways: the mating connectors must be compatible to the plug end, and the resistance of the plug cap must be the correct value for the installed spark plug. Resistance values in the plug and cap optimize the spark, so it is important to check the plug designation and verify its type (resistance or non-resistance) before measuring the cap resistance.

Types of Spark Plugs

Figure 5-3-6 shows the two types of plugs found in LSA engines. The non-shielded design is familiar in automotive applications and has become popular in lower-power rated aircraft engines. The shielded design has been used as a standard in aircraft powerplants and has the advantage of requiring a threaded connection to attach the plug lead.

The inspection of the spark plugs can frequently reveal a great deal about the health of an engine. The appearance of the electrode-end of the plug will often show the health of the combustion process, and indicate what, if any, changes should be made to improve engine performance.

Spark Plug Condition Inspection

An examination of the spark plug should consider the above conditions as well as normal wear that may result in plug servicing or replacement. Electrodes will erode with time, requiring them to be regapped to the specs provided by the engine manufacturer. An enlarged gap will create more resistance in the circuit, possibly causing the spark plug to fail because a path of less resistance has been found in the wiring circuit. Spark plugs should be replaced if the electrode erosion requires a significant adjustment to achieve the proper gap.

Carbon build up around the spark plug and plug hole will frequently make installation and removal of the plug difficult. For this reason, it is recommended to pass a *cleanout tap* through the plug hole if binding is felt as the plug is screwed into the hole.

Figure 5-3-7. Proper technique for removing spark plugs

When removing spark plugs, it is necessary to use a deep socket and support the socket with one hand so that when torque is applied through the wrench, the socket will not misalign with the plug. Figure 5-3-7 shows the proper technique for removing spark plugs; misalignment of the wrench can damage the plug.

> **CAUTION:** *Always remove and install plugs on a cold engine.*

Due to thermal expansion, it may be very difficult to remove a spark plug on a hot engine. After removal, the plugs are carefully examined and stored in a tray or cardboard box with holes cut into it so that the plug electrodes will not be damaged. See Figure 5-3-8. The gap is easily changed on a plug, so avoiding any con-

Figure 5-3-8. A spark plug storage tray should be used to avoid damaging the plugs.

Figure 5-3-9. Carbon soot built up on a spark plug

Figure 5-3-10. A properly functioning spark plug

Figure 5-3-11. A spark plug with whitish lead compound deposits

tact of the electrodes is critical until an adjustment has to be made. If the plug is dropped on a hard floor, it should not be re-used.

Carbon fouling. Figure 5-3-9 shows a plug with a black, velvety appearance indicating that carbon soot has built up on the plug, usually caused by a mixture that is too rich. A plug with a sooty deposit can be caused by a rich mixture at cruise power or idle power, depending on the carburetor mixture settings. It may be necessary to perform diagnostics on the engine at multiple speeds to determine the source of the rich combustion mixture so that proper corrective action can be taken.

On both two and four-stroke engines, the carburetor function is nearly identical and the items to check for in the case of rich mixture would be:

- Idle jet setting

- Idle speed setting

- Worn or improperly functioning main jet or needle

- Carburetor float is sticking

- Leaking primer system on carburetor

- Choke is sticking, or intake air is being restricted

Oil fouling. If ignition is intermittent or not happening at all, the plug and the rest of the combustion chamber will become wet with unburned gasoline which can further reduce the likelihood of proper ignition. A plug which is oily because crankcase oil has migrated into the combustion chamber will also cause a short. This can happen during periods of inactivity. An engine that is frequently hard to start may have an oil fouling problem caused by oil leaking into the combustion chamber from the valve guides (top end) or past the piston (bottom end) while the engine is not running. Two stroke engines that are running rich will tend to leave an oily residue in the cylinder either during start-up or shut-down, and this can make starting difficult. A plug which is shorting out because of oil or gasoline will generally correct itself if the engine is able to run on the reduced number of plugs, providing a drying effect and restoring the ignition function.

Lead fouling. The use of 100 LL fuel in an engine can cause lead fouling, or the accumulation of solid lead compounds on the spark plug electrodes which results in a short and no spark. This condition frequently happens if the engine is idled for a long period of time, or during cruise at lean mixture settings. Since some degree of lead fouling may be unavoidable, the affected plugs need to be thoroughly cleaned so that further accumulations do not worsen the condition.

Figure 5-3-12. Starter with a Bendix drive

Plug Inspection Procedures

1. Be sure the plug is of the approved type, as indicated by the applicable manufacturer's instructions.

2. Check both ends of the plug for nicked or cracked threads and any indication of cracks in the nose insulator.

3. Inspect the inside of the shielding barrel for cracks in the barrel insulator, and the center electrode contact for rust and foreign material that might cause poor electrical contact.

4. Inspect the spark plug gasket. A gasket that has been excessively flattened, scarred, dented or distorted by previous use must not be used. Used, serviceable, copper spark plug gaskets should be annealed prior to reinstallation. When the thermocouple gasket is used, do not use an additional gasket.

5. Check the top of the plug for the proper cap or bare thread, as specified by the engine manufacturer. Spark plugs come in many different configurations designed for compatibility with the plug lead, and the proper interface is necessary for electrical continuity.

Manufacturers commonly discourage screw-on end caps for the plug as they tend to wear and break off. The preferred plug end is therefore a bare thread or a solid cap.

A properly functioning plug should have a uniform, brownish tinge shown in Figure 5-3-10. For engines with a single carburetor, one sooty plug would indicate a bad plug or faulty ignition system. If both plugs are sooty, then the carburetion and air system should be checked.

If the plugs are whitish with lead compound deposits on them as shown in Figure 5-3-11,

suspect that a lean mixture exists. A lean mixture can have numerous sources:

- Manifold leaks
- Lack of fuel
- Incorrect carburetor float setting
- Improper engine cooling

These plugs have been operated at elevated temperatures and may show damage in the form of melted, eroded or deformed electrodes as well. When replacing spark plugs, follow the manufacturer's recommendation on torque and the use of anti-seize compound.

Starter Inspection

The starters on LSA aircraft are usually geared or direct drive, series wound DC motors. They deliver a high torque through a pinion gear which engages to the ring gear on the motor. The ring gear is a large gear found either behind the propeller (Lycoming), or on the back of the engine (Rotax and Jabiru). Part of the inspection of the motor should include a check for excessive wear in the pinion and the mechanism that forces the pinion out into the ring gear when the motor is engaged. The starter mounting hardware should also be inspected for tightness.

Many starters use a torque sensing design called the Bendix drive that engages the pinion with the ring gear as soon as the motor begins turning. Figure 5-3-12 shows a Bendix drive. A starter motor will wear prematurely if wiring prevents the full battery voltage from reaching the motor. Excessive arcing in the brushes and overheating will result if the motor fails to turn over at full speed due to low voltage, so a thorough inspection of the wiring to the starter is important. Particular attention should be paid to the ground

Figure 5-3-13. Alternator/generator commonly found on LSA

or return path since high resistance here will cause a low voltage condition in the starter.

The ring gear should be inspected for signs of cracking and excessive wear from the pinion.

Alternator Inspection

The alternator/generator found on LSA may be a belt-driven unit, a self contained unit mounted to the accessory case through a frangible link, or an integral unit that is part of the motor design. Most integral units not only generate power for the aircraft, but they also function as the power source for the ignition system (Figure 5-3-13). This has the advantage of saving weight by using a common rotor (flywheel) for both electrical systems.

The inspection of the electrical system should start with the wiring, to ensure there are no breaks or burned through areas that may cause a short. The function of the alternator/generator should be checked by running the engine up to operating speed and then turning on all electrical systems so that a full load condition is created. No circuit breakers should open, and even though the battery may start to discharge slightly, the bus voltage should not fluctuate.

If the alternator is belt driven, the belt tension should be checked to the manufacturer's rec-

ommended specifications. Belts loosen with time, and a periodic adjustment may be necessary. Check for cracking on the inside of the belt, caused by heat and age, with replacement recommended at the first sign that cracks have developed. For all self-contained units, the condition of the bearings should be checked by moving the rotor slowly and listening for bearing noise.

Section 4

The Intake System

The air intake system on many LSA is as simple as an air filter mounted to the intake side of the carburetor. On tightly cowled designs, there may be ducting that routes intake air from a high pressure point on the airframe to an air cleaner and then to the carburetor air intake. These systems should be inspected for signs of collapsed tubing, abrasion or degradation of the air ducts that would result in leakage.

Air cleaners sometimes have regular replacement intervals, or can be rejuvenated by cleaning and applying an air cleaner oil on them to trap dirt. The K & N Air Filters, common on Bing carburetors, can be easily serviced and the manufacturer's recommendations on this procedure should be followed. These filters have a tab located on them for safety wiring, which should be used.

Carburetor Overview

After passing through the air filter, air is routed to the carburetor. The purpose of the carburetor is to provide the proper air/fuel ratio mixture to optimize the combustion process. The pilot can also control the mixture entering the engine which will regulate its power. The schematic shown in Figure 5-4-1 represents the basic operation of a carburetor with fuel entering the air stream in a place of higher velocity due to a restriction built into the intake barrel, called a *venturi*. Bernoulli's principle states that pressure will drop as the velocity of a fluid increases, and at the narrowest part of the venturi, we can expect a lower pressure to exist. The fuel from the float bowl is sucked into the venturi at a rate that is proportional to the speed of the intake flow, thus providing a relatively uniform control of the mixture entering the engine.

This simple schematic ignores additional fuel and air entry points within the barrel that must occur to achieve acceptable operation over a range of engine speeds, operating conditions and atmospheric pressures. These systems include:

- Main metering
- Idling
- Accelerating
- Mixture cutoff
- Idle cutoff
- Power enrichment or economizer

Each of these systems has a definite function. It may act alone or with one or more of the others.

Main metering system. The *main metering system* supplies fuel to the engine at all speeds above idling. The fuel discharged by this system is determined by the drop in pressure in the venturi throat.

Idling system. A separate system is necessary for idling because the main metering system is unreliable at very low engine speeds. At low speed, the throttle is nearly closed. As a result, the velocity of the air through the venturi is low and there is little drop in pressure. Consequently, the differential pressure is not sufficient to operate the main metering system, and no fuel is discharged from the system. Therefore, most

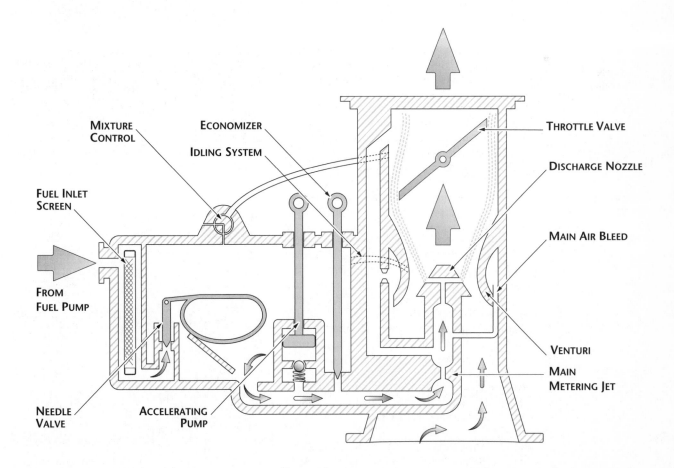

Figure 5-4-1. Basic operation of a carburetor

Figure 5-4-2. Typical carburetor used with a four-stroke engine with manual mixture control

carburetors have an *idling system* to supply fuel to the engine at low engine speeds.

Accelerating system. The *accelerating system* supplies extra fuel during increases in engine power. When the throttle is opened to obtain more power from the engine, the airflow through the carburetor increases. The main metering system then increases the fuel discharge. During sudden acceleration, however, the increase in airflow is so rapid that there is a slight time lag before the increase in fuel discharge is sufficient to provide the correct mixture ratio with the new airflow. By supplying extra fuel during this period, the accelerating system prevents a temporary leaning-out of the mixture and gives smooth acceleration.

Mixture-control system. The *mixture-control system* determines the ratio of fuel to air in the mixture. By means of a cockpit control, the operator can select the mixture ratio to suit operating conditions. In addition to these manual controls, many carburetors have automatic mixture controls so that the fuel/air ratio, once it is selected, does not change with variations in air density. This is necessary because, as the airplane climbs and the atmospheric pressure decreases, there is a corresponding decrease in the weight of air passing through the induction system. The volume, however, remains constant and, since it is the volume of airflow which determines the pressure drop at the throat of the venturi, the carburetor tends to meter the same amount of fuel to this thin air as to the dense air at sea level. Thus, the natural tendency is for the mixture to become richer as the airplane gains altitude. The automatic mixture control prevents this by decreasing the rate of fuel discharge to compensate for the decrease in air density.

Idle-cutoff system. The carburetor has an *idle-cutoff system* so that the fuel can be shut off to stop the engine. This system, incorporated in the manual mixture control, stops the fuel dis-

charge from the carburetor completely when the mixture-control lever is set to the idle-cutoff position. In any discussion of the idle-cutoff system, this question usually comes up: Why is an aircraft engine stopped by shutting off the fuel rather than by turning off the ignition? To answer this question, it is necessary to examine the results of both methods. If the ignition is turned off with the carburetor still supplying fuel, fresh fuel/air mixture continues to pass through the induction system to the cylinders while the engine is coasting to a stop. If the engine is excessively hot, this combustible mixture may be ignited by local hot spots within the combustion chambers, and the engine may keep on running or kick backward. Again, the mixture may pass out of the cylinders unburned but be ignited in the hot exhaust manifold. More often, however, the engine will come to an apparently normal stop but have a combustible mixture in the induction passages, the cylinders and the exhaust system. This is an unsafe condition, since the engine may kick over after it

Figure 5-4-3. Bing carburetor set up for a single lever power control.

Figure 5-4-4. Residue or varnish on internal parts in a two-stroke carburetor

Photo courtesy of SoLo Aviation

has been stopped and seriously injure anyone near the propeller. On the other hand, when the engine is shut down by means of the idle-cutoff system, the spark plugs continue to ignite the fuel/air mixture until the fuel discharge from the carburetor ceases. This alone should prevent the engine from coming to a stop with a combustible mixture in the cylinders.

Some engine manufacturers suggest that, just before the propeller stops turning, the throttle be opened wide so that the pistons can pump fresh air through the induction system, the cylinders and the exhaust system as an added precaution against accidental kick-over. After the engine has come to a complete stop, the ignition switch is turned to the OFF position.

Power-enrichment system. The *power-enrichment system* automatically increases the richness of the mixture during high-power operation. In this way, it enables the variation in fuel/air ratio necessary to fit different operating conditions. Remember that, at cruising speeds, a lean mixture is desirable for reasons of economy while, at high-power output, the mixture must be rich to obtain maximum power and to aid in cooling the engine. The power-enrichment system automatically brings about the necessary change in the fuel/air ratio. Essentially, it is a valve that is closed at cruising speeds and opens to supply extra fuel to the mixture during high-power operation. Although it increases the fuel flow at high power, the power-enrichment system is actually a fuel-saving device. Without this system, it would be necessary to operate the engine on a rich mixture over the complete power range. The mixture would then be richer than necessary at cruising speed to ensure safe operation at maximum power. The power-enrichment system is sometimes called an *economizer* or a *power compensator*.

Although the various systems have been discussed separately, the carburetor functions as a unit. The fact that one system is in operation does not necessarily prevent another from functioning simultaneously. At the same time that the main metering system is discharging fuel in proportion to the airflow, the mixture-control system determines whether the resultant mixture will be rich or lean. If the throttle is suddenly opened wide, the accelerating and power-enrichment systems act to add fuel to that already being discharged by the main metering system.

Carburetor Inspection

Figure 5-4-2 shows a typical carburetor for a four-stroke engine with manual mixture control. The carburetors on two and four stroke engines share similar features such as the throttle, needle jet, float and float needle valve which all act to regulate the mixture into the

Figure 5-4-5. Cable housing adjustments may be necessary to remove slack in the system that develops with time

throttle body. The carburetor is a sensitive part of the engine, especially when fuel flow is regulated by a barometric device that senses atmospheric pressure and controls the mixture automatically. Such systems allow for "single lever" power control, reducing the pilot workload in operating the engine. Figure 5-4-3 shows a Bing carburetor that operates on this principle.

In the case of two stroke carburetors, removal of the float bowl and an inspection of the condition of the inside of the bowl and the main jet body is required since the gas/oil mix can leave a residue or varnish on these internal parts (Figure 5-4-4). If this builds up in sufficient quantity, it will adversely affect the air/fuel ratio. Any time the engine sits for a period of time, this bowl should be emptied to prevent the formation and accumulation of varnish. An oily residue can also accumulate on the bottom of the intake portion of the carburetor due to gas/oil mix continuing to flow into the carburetor after the engine has been shut down. The gasoline will evaporate, but the oil will accumulate and this can potentially clog passageways and vents.

If the engine inspection reveals a rich or lean mixture, the removal of the float bowl will also allow a diagnostic check of the regulating function of the float. For the Bing carburetors, the engine can be run briefly and then shut down while simultaneously closing the fuel shut-off valve. Removing the float bowl and comparing the fuel level to the manufacturer's specifications will indicate if the float is functioning properly.

Carburetors have an airflow regulating device called the throttle which governs the amount of air/fuel mixture entering the engine. These devices can either take the form of a butterfly valve that is actuated by a lever on the side of the throttle body, or a slide valve that is actuated by a top-mounted cable. Slide valves are common on two cycle engines, and butterfly valves are more common on four cycles. During an inspection, this moving part should

Figure 5-4-7. Integral jet needle held in place by a clip

Photo courtesy of SoLo Aviation

Figure 5-4-6. Slide valve from a two-stroke carburetor

Figure 5-4-8. Boot couplings must be examined for cracks under the metal retaining band.

be inspected for binding or looseness that may be due to wear or improper adjustment.

An inspection of the cables and springs that are attached to the throttle and other engine controls should be made to ensure proper routing and function without binding or restriction to movement. Since the engine can vibrate signif-

Figure 5-4-9. Clear tubes feed atmospheric pressure to the float chamber on a Bing carburetor.

icantly on start-up and shut-down, cable routing should be checked to make sure a wear situation does not develop as the engine moves. Cable housing adjustments may be necessary over time as slight movement of the housing and cable can occur. (Figure 5-4-5, previous page). Be particularly careful in inspecting cable housings as the idle speed can be affected by this housing adjustment if the carburetor return spring acts to close the throttle. When retarded, the engine should idle based on settings made at the carburetor and not by residual tension in the throttle cable caused by an improper adjustment.

A small amount of slack (less than 1/16 inch but greater than 1/32 inch) should be observed in the cable when the throttle is fully retarded. Likewise, springs on 9xx series Rotax carburetors are usually set up to hold the throttle wide open, and when the throttle is fully advanced the carburetor stop should be encountered before the throttle control stop.

Two-stroke carburetors commonly contain a slide valve (Figure 5-4-6) that has an integral jet needle held in place by a clip as shown in Figure 5-4-7. The needle has been found to loosen and rotate in Bing carburetor installations, and numerous publications including a Service Bulletin have recommended fixes to the problem. Any inspection of a Bing carburetor should examine the integrity of the needle held captive in the clip, and if not already done, the Service Bulletin should be complied with. Failure of the jet needle will result in sudden power loss.

A carburetor typically has jet adjustment screws which are used to control air flow or fuel flow at either high or low speeds. These may require adjustment if the engine is observed to be running rich or lean, evident in the condition of the spark plugs. Some engine manufacturers recommend that jets be changed if operation of the engine is routinely from a field that does not represent standard conditions, i.e., 59° F and sea level elevation. In addition to adjusting the jets, the idle stop on the throttle lever or slide valve must be positioned to give the proper engine idle speed.

CAUTION: *Geared motors will suffer damage if the idle speed is too low.*

Many engines become difficult to start if the idle speed is set too high.

Carburetors on LSA engines are frequently attached to the intake manifold through a compliant sleeve that absorbs engine vibration. These boot couplings (Figure 5-4-8) must be examined for cracks by removing the carburetor and metal retaining band to get a clear view of the highest stress areas which are most likely to crack. It will be necessary to squeeze the rubber sleeve to reveal hidden cracks which can lead to a lean mixture at best, and worst, complete failure of the carburetor attachment to the engine. Any cracks that appear on close examination are cause for replacement.

All flexible tubes attached to the carburetor should be inspected for wear, perforation, cracking, heat damage, and improper installation or routing. The Bing two stroke carburetor requires a vent tube attached to two side ports which feed atmospheric air into the float chamber (shown as the clear vertical tube in Figure 5-4-9). These lines ideally will channel the static pressure from the engine intake (air cleaner) to the float chamber, and if they are routed anywhere away from the intake, the resulting mixture can be significantly impacted. For instance, vent lines that end up near areas of high velocity air will experience lower pressures due to Bernoulli's principle. Proper routing and function of these static lines should be carefully inspected.

When multiple carburetors are installed, it is necessary to synchronize them to ensure equal power is achieved on all cylinders. Synchronization starts with the most basic mechanical synchronization: an inspection of the cables and throttle valves to ensure operation is uniform. The inspection continues by measuring the idle opening or full power opening of the slide or butterfly valves on the carburetors, depending on the orientation of the return spring. Figure 5-4-6 shows a slide valve with the small opening needed to allow the idle mixture to pass through.

With the throttle retarded, the slide valve rests on a large tapered screw that enters the throttle body from the side, and a small amount of slack will be observed in the cable housing. See Figure 5-4-5. The idle screw is adjusted to give the same idle setting opening on all carburetors; an opening dictated by the desired idle speed. Fine adjustment can be achieved by matching EGTs by 15° F.

With the engine shut down, the throttle is advanced to a mid-power setting and a bore gauge or similar device is used to match the openings on all carburetors. Adjustment are made with the cable housing adjusting screw located on the top of the carburetor. Again, when the engine is running, the EGTs can be used to fine-tune these adjustments. After the throttle cables are set, the oil injection pump control lever should be checked for its settings against reference marks.

Dual carburetor installations may also have a cross-feeding compensating tube that serves to equalize manifold pressure between the intake systems, shown in Figure 5-4-10. If the tube is

EQUALIZING MANIFOLD

Figure 5-4-10. Dual carberetor crossfeed equalizing manifold

Figure 5-4-11. The cable splitter must be firmly mounted

disconnected and plugged on both ends, there should be no noticeable reduction in RPM, otherwise an unbalance between the carburetors exists. Rotax has a pressure calibration procedure for the 9xx series motors which requires this tube to be disconnected and pressure gages installed on each side. The manufacturer's procedure on pneumatic synchronization should be followed in this case.

Moving the inspection from the engine up the cables leads to the cable splitter, which takes a single pilot-operated cable and creates multiple cables for multiple carburetors and an oil injection pump, if installed. The splitter, shown in Figure 5-4-11 must be firmly mounted and operate without binding. Continuing to the

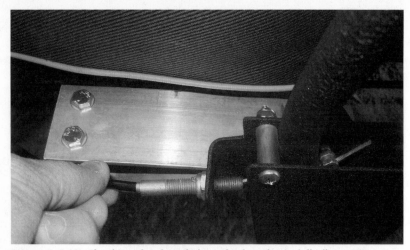

Figure 5-4-12. Checking the throttle lever for freeplay in full idle postion.

Figure 5-5-1. Exhaust system flexible joint with springs

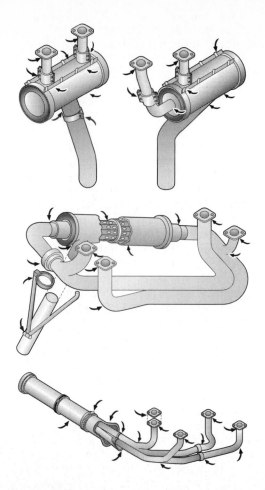

Figure 5-5-2. Places to inspect for leakage in an exhaust system

cockpit, the throttle lever should be checked for a small amount of freeplay when the throttle is moved to full idle (Figure 5-4-12), or full advance, depending on the arrangement of the return spring on the carburetor.

Section 5

The Exhaust System

The exhaust system on an internal combustion engine routes combustion byproducts from the engine to a safe location away from the airframe. Usually a muffler is included in the exhaust system to reduce the noise generated from the sudden rush of exhaust gases outside of the engine. Exhaust systems have joints that are not rigid, but are designed to flex so that the vibration of the engine does not cause a fracture. This requirement leads to several unique designs that allow some relative motion in the

system without leaking gases that would be dangerous in the cockpit. Figure 5-5-1 shows a typical flexible joint that uses springs to hold the elements of the system together.

While an exhaust system can withstand temperatures on the order of 1,400° F, it frequently has a shroud that allows cooling air to pass over it, and this can double as a heat exchanger for cabin heat. Since air that is destined for the cockpit passes right over the exhaust system, it is extremely important that an inspection of the system includes all possible exhaust escape paths that may result in tainted cabin air. Carbon monoxide, a deadly gas in sufficient doses, is a byproduct of combustion that must be prevented from ever entering the cabin.

During the inspection, disassembly of all or part of the exhaust system (manifold, muffler, tailpipe) is recommended to inspect for burn-through and pin holes that may become larger with continued operation. Joints should be carefully examined for signs of exhaust leakage, usually indicated by a tan streak if the engine is burning 100 LL gasoline. Flexible exhaust joints should be lubricated with a heat resistant anti-seize compound, which acts to seal the exhaust system and also allows for

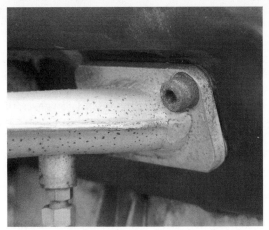

Figure 5-5-3. Exhaust studs must be replaced before they are impossible to remove

Figure 5-5-4. Retaining springs with safety wire

relative movement between the parts. Figure 5-5-2 shows exhaust systems with arrows indicating places to inspect for leakage.

The muffler usually has baffles which disperse the energy of the exhaust stream, quieting the noise of the engine. The disadvantage to this system is that if the baffles fail, they may obstruct the flow of gases exiting the engine. This can lead to a sudden power loss. During the inspection, it is critical to inspect as much of the interior of the muffler as possible for signs of baffle weakness or breakage. The use of a borescope is recommended to reach into the tailpipe and up into the muffler for this job.

Removal of the exhaust manifold on a two stroke engine is highly recommended since the cylinder inspection will be considerably more thorough. Two stroke engines typically have carbon deposits that should not exceed 0.02 in. thick, and this maximum thickness applies to the exhaust system as well. Even if the exhaust system on the engine is not removed, the replacement of the nuts or studs holding the exhaust manifold onto the engine is recommended since these will corrode with time if they are steel. Figure 5-5-3 shows an exhaust stud that needs to be replaced before it becomes impossible to remove.

Follow the manufacturer's recommendations on retaining spring replacement and safety wiring, a critical item since the loss of a spring can damage the propeller on pusher configurations. Figure 5-5-4 shows retaining springs with safety wire passing through the center of the springs. Springs are now available with holes on either end for safety wiring, so that no part of the spring will depart the aircraft if it fails. Manufacturers also recommend retorquing the exhaust manifold studs on a periodic basis, and the torque values and intervals should be observed. Finally, time in service should be noted, and replacement of the exhaust system should be performed if required by the manufacturer.

Section 6
Engine Cooling

Liquid cooled systems. Engines that have a radiator circulate coolant through all or part of the engine to transfer heat from the engine. Liquid cooled engines have a more uniform temperature distribution than air cooled engines, and this allows the engine to be designed with tighter tolerances and clearances. This usually translates into less oil consumption and smoother operation, but at the expense of more complexity. Some engines such as the Rotax 9xx series are uniquely designed with hybrid cooling, where the cylinders are air cooled, the cylinder heads are liquid cooled, and the engine oil is additionally cooled with an oil cooler. Figure 5-6-1 shows the top-end cooling system of a Rotax 912. Care should be given to

Figure 5-6-1. Rotax 912 top-end cooling system using both liquid and air

Figure 5-6-2. Oil reservoir for the water pump/ rotary valve attached to the engine

inspecting a liquid cooled system, for failure of hoses or seals or a significant leakage event can result in engine damage and possible catastrophic failure.

Examine for signs of coolant leakage on the outside of the engine. Generally, the coolant system will operate at a higher pressure than atmospheric and this can force coolant outside or into other parts of the engine. On the Rotax 532 and 582 engines, an oil lubrication system that services the water pump/rotary valve drive system will show signs of seal failure if the oil reservoir becomes opaque and lighter in color. This is due to coolant leaking into the oil reservoir. The reservoir in this case is a small plastic bottle that is either attached to the engine or airframe, shown in Figure 5-6-2. In the case of the Rotax 9xx series engines, the engine oil system services the water pump and so the engine oil may show signs of contamination in the event of seal failure.

Bolts that pass through a water jacket may begin to leak if they were not properly treated during installation. Bolts or nuts used on a cylinder head may have an integral widened, flat area

with concentric ridges that seal when a grease or RTV is applied. Inspect for leakage around all bolted fittings passing through the water jacket.

Failure of the head seal around the top of the cylinder can result in either the cooling system being pressurized by combustion gases, or coolant leaking into the combustion chamber. If the cooling system becomes pressurized, there will be an excess amount of coolant forced into the overflow bottle. Leakage into the cylinder is evident by water vapor in the exhaust, usually more prevalent during start-up and low power operation. The smell of coolant will be present in the exhaust if this occurs.

The radiator, expansion tank, water pump and associated hardware should be inspected for leaks and evidence of damage. Hose clamps should be checked for tightness, and hoses should be inspected for bulges or soft spots that would indicate heat damage. The radiator can have damage to some of the fins without compromising its function, however if the thin vertical tubes are bent or scratched, the radiator should be replaced. Mounting tabs should be inspected for fatigue cracks which may develop if the vibration environment is high. A typical radiator installation is shown in Figure 5-6-3, next page.

The coolant should be verified that it meets the manufacturer's recommendations. Discolored or thickened coolant must be replaced, and the proper levels should be checked.

> **CAUTION:** *Never work on the cooling system until the engine has cooled down to ambient temperature.*

Serious burns can result from the system which is under pressure and hot. Coolant is rated by its boiling temperature, and problems

Figure 5-6-3. A radiator installation

with Rotax engines developing hot spots on the heads due to localized boiling have resulted in a need to use higher boiling point coolants. Since the use of these more expensive coolants is driven by high head temperatures, an operator that never sees these high temps would not have to change coolants.

The Rotax 582 and 9xx series engines have an expansion tank mounted above the rest of the cooling system which vents coolant into the overflow bottle and regulates the system pressure. These tanks should be inspected for proper sealing of the cap, and a visual inspection of the pressure regulating mechanism inside the cap should verify that the relief valve works. If a replacement cap is needed, the regulating pressure should be based on the manufacturer's specification.

The overflow bottle should be inspected for damage and proper venting based on the manufacturer's specifications. Secure mounting and safety wiring should be verified as well.

Air cooled systems. Engines that are air cooled usually have a means of forcing air around the fins of the heads and cylinders to accelerate heat transfer. Historically, this has been done by cowling the engine so that some of the prop wash, or incident air will be routed over the engine in an effective manner. Modern two stroke engines also have self contained fans that blow air over the top end of the engine, providing a more uniform cooling effect.

For engines with a belt driven fan, it is important to inspect for belt wear and looseness that may have to be corrected with a new belt, as shown in Figure 5-6-4. A loose belt can begin to slip, and this will result in total failure if the belt overheats and breaks. Some manufacturers allow belt tension to be adjusted with shims placed in the fan sheave, but this only provides a limited adjust-

Figure 5-6-4. Belt wear and looseness is corrected by replacing the belt.

Photo courtesty of SoLo Aviation

1. OIL SUCTION SCREEN
2. OIL TEMP. SENDER
3. OIL PUMP
4. OIL RESERVOIR
5. OIL COOLER
6. OIL FILTER
7. OIL TANK VENT
8. OIL PRESSURE PORT

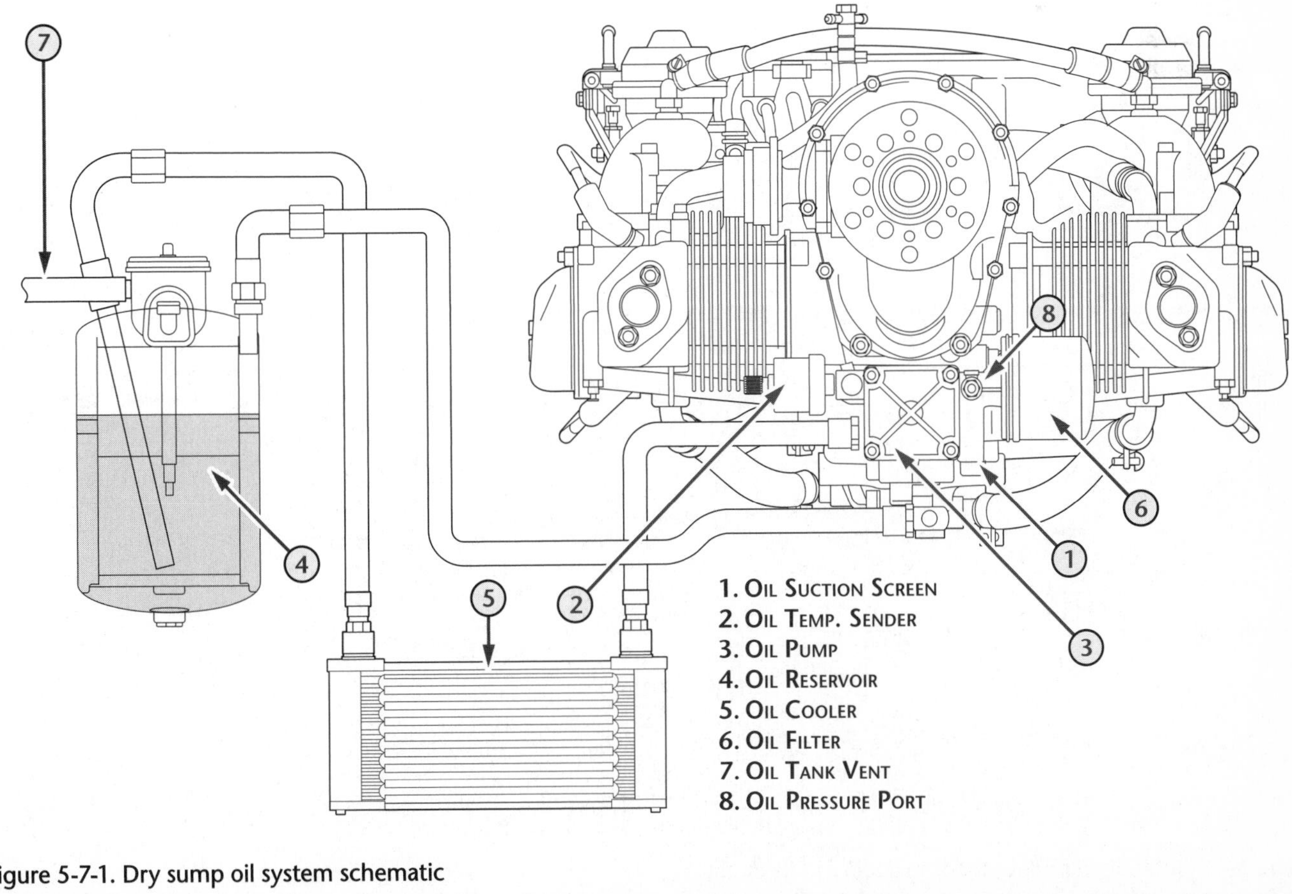

Figure 5-7-1. Dry sump oil system schematic

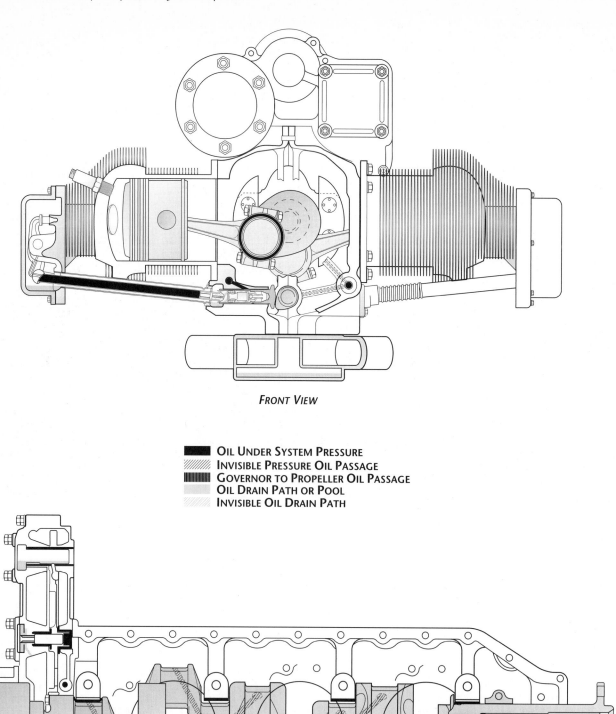

FRONT VIEW

OIL UNDER SYSTEM PRESSURE
INVISIBLE PRESSURE OIL PASSAGE
GOVERNOR TO PROPELLER OIL PASSAGE
OIL DRAIN PATH OR POOL
INVISIBLE OIL DRAIN PATH

SIDE VIEW

Figure 5-7-2. Interior oil routing paths in a four stroke engine

ment. Consult the engine manufacturer for the proper technique in determining belt tension and setting the tension to the correct value.

The condition of the fan bearings should be assessed by carefully listening to the fan as it is rotated slowly. Never rotate the fan by the blades if the belt is engaged, since they are not designed to handle the torque required to turn over the engine.

Section 7

Lubrication Systems

Four stroke engine. The engine lubrication system acts to reduce friction among moving parts, conduct heat away, protect parts from corrosion, and reduce shock loading by providing a cushioning effect between moving parts. In addition, the use of a viscous fluid such as oil will help to seal the piston against the cylinder in the compression and combustion strokes, where high pressures are generated.

Oil has always been a part of internal combustion engines, and advances in aircraft engine lubrication have mainly involved improvements to the chemical composition of oil. *Multi-viscosity* oils are designed to have a more stable viscosity over a range of operating temperatures, reducing stresses and improving the engine's lubrication properties. Viscosity ratings are usually based on the SAE standard, and the specifications for the engine should be referenced to select the proper viscosity oil based on temperatures and operating conditions. As an example, Rotax recommends SAE 20W-50 oil for a range of temperatures from -5° C to 40° C. An SAE 5W-40 is recommended if the temperatures are as low as -30° C.

In addition to viscosity, a service category of the oil must be considered. The American Petroleum Institute (API) service categories are used to select an oil that meets the needs of the engine manufacturer. As an example, an "SL" category oil is designed to provide better high-temperature deposit control and lower oil consumption. The engine manufacturer will specify the API category of oil that should be used.

Some engine oils are specifically designed for air cooled engines, which have larger clearances and more temperature variation during operation than a water cooled engine. It is important to observe the manufacturer's recommendations on oil for this reason, as aircraft oils are designed specifically for air-cooled aircraft engines. Jabiru, Lycoming and Continental Aircraft engines all require oils specifically designed for the air-cooled aircraft engine.

CAUTION: *Do not run automotive oils in these engines.*

A typical dry sump oil system is shown in Figure 5-7-1 (page 5-29). The term dry sump refers to the fact that the oil reservoir is external to the engine, and the bottom of the engine serves as a collector of oil that has been pressure-fed through the engine. Larger aircraft engines use a dry sump system, but Rotax has also chosen a dry sump system for their 9xx series engines. Wet sump systems are commonly employed in Lycoming and Continental aircraft engines in the 100 hp.–350 hp. range. The advantage of a wet sump system is that the oil system is simplified by integrating the reservoir into the bottom of the engine.

Figure 5-7-3. Whistle slot in the crankcase breather

All aircraft lubrication systems have an oil pump that takes oil in from a reservoir, usually through a filtering screen, and forces oil under pressure around the engine through *galleys*, or passageways drilled into the engine block. Main crankshaft bearings are lubricated by oil that is pressurized into the space between the crankshaft and the bearing support blocks, providing a cushion of oil that eliminates metal-to-metal contact. Oil is also directed into the top end of the engine where the valves are located either by using the pushrod as an oil conduit, or by using a separate external oil line routed to the engine head. Figure 5-7-2 shows interior oil routing paths in a four stroke engine.

The oil system of an engine should be inspected for leaks and proper operation. The exterior of the engine should be carefully inspected for evidence of oil leakage, through seals or a failure of lines or galleys. Very small amounts of oil seepage (dampness) from bolted interfaces, such as the cylinder/block interface may not be an immediate problem but should be monitored carefully for increased flow. Larger leaks that result in drops of oil forming on the bottom of the engine should be immediately addressed since this could indicate an imminent failure.

Oil leakage should not be confused with the function of the oil breather tube that is connected to the crankcase and vents the crankcase so that excessive pressure does not build up. This tube might show evidence of oil passing through it, which is normal. This tube should be checked for a small hole, or "whistle slot," that is located somewhere in the engine compartment and vents the crankcase if the bottom of the tube ices up in freezing conditions (Figure 5-7-3). Serious engine damage can occur if there is not provision for crankcase venting (of course, not a problem for two stroke engines).

Figure 5-7-4. Hoses with wire wrap applied to prevent collapsing when the oil is cold and viscous.

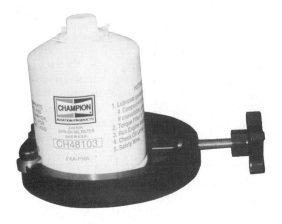

Figure 5-7-5. Oil filter cutter

All hoses associated with the lubrication system should be inspected for wear, abrasion, kinking, heat damage and incorrect attachment that might cause restrictions to the oil flow. These include hoses to the reservoir tank, the oil pump, the crankcase vent hose, and hoses that service the engine heads and any accessories requiring engine oil. Hoses that have negative pressure on them (vacuum), such as between the reservoir tank and the oil pump commonly have a wire wrap applied to prevent collapsing when the oil is cold and viscous. These should be inspected to ensure they are in fact located on the suction lines, and that they are properly positioned on the line, shown in Figure 5-7-4. For engines with an oil cooler, the cooler fittings should be inspected for leakage and the cooler tubes should not be bent or nicked. Minor damage to the heat transfer fins is acceptable as long as the tubes have no signs of damage.

Oil Filter. The oil filter should be removed and inspected by following the manufacturer's recommendations on opening the filter to access the filtering element. An oil filter cutter is shown in Figure 5-7-5. This allows the removal of the filtering element for inspection. By carefully examining the filter element under good lighting conditions, metal particles and other debris that can indicate excessive engine wear can be detected. Particles that may be found in the filter element include steel, bronze or aluminum chips, silver of bearing material, and the remains of sealing compound. The manufacturer will usually provide guidelines on determining what is acceptable to find in the filter without overhauling the engine. This inspection can be complemented by performing an oil analysis on a regular basis, usually coinciding with oil changes. There are several companies that offer oil analysis services, usually as simple as mailing a small bottle of engine oil to the lab for a spectrographic analysis, shown in Figure 5-7-6. Trends in metal content found during analysis are much more important than absolute values, and this should be noted over the course of several analyses.

Proper oil quantity should be checked and the oil consumption noted, again to find anomalies in the normal rate of oil consumption that would indicate a problem. When replacing an oil filter, be sure to use the type recommended by the manufacturer, since an engine warranty can be voided otherwise.

Some engines also contain a magnetic plug in the bottom of the engine. This should be inspected for the accumulation of metallic particles. Like the filter element, the manufacturer will indicate what is acceptable and what is excessive.

During a functional test of the engine, oil pressure should be monitored for correct values during start-up and after the engine has reached its normal operating temperature. Oil pressure on a cold engine may take a while to build, because the higher viscosity of the oil causes a lag in pressure monitoring at the pressure gauge. Other causes of low oil pressure during start up include air in the oil pump after an oil change, requiring "venting" of the lubrication system. This can occur on dry sump engines where the oil pump is remote to the oil reservoir. See the manufacturer's recommended procedure on venting if it is required. Rotax suggests that oil pressure should rise to at least 2 bar (30 p.s.i.) within 10 seconds after start-up, and if this value is not achieved, the engine should be immediately shut down. A low oil pressure can be the result of problems in the engine or the oil pressure gauge itself, and this should be considered when troubleshooting. Most engines allow some adjustment of the oil pressure by manipulating an oil pressure regulator on the engine.

Possible causes of low oil pressure:

- Low oil quantity
- Malfunctioning pressure sensor
- Malfunctioning pressure relief valve
- Clogged intake screen or other restrictions in the system
- Incorrect oil viscosity
- Dry oil pump

Oil temperature is regulated by a thermostat which usually directs engine oil to the oil cooler once a minimum temperature is achieved. Improper oil temperatures during operation can be traced to one of several factors:

- Malfunctioning thermostat
- Blocked oil cooler, possibly due to debris that has lodged in the cooler from the system.
- Engine mixture set too lean
- Insufficient cooling air on oil cooler or engine
- Oil screen at pick-up is clogged (also will cause low oil pressure)

Two stroke engines. Two stroke engines do not have a formal lubrication system since the fuel serves as the lubricant in the crankcase. Most two stroke engines run on a 50:1 mixture of gasoline and oil, providing enough lubrication to service the crank bearings and the sliding friction of the pistons in the cylinders. However, because the viscosity of the mix is extremely low and there is no pressure lubrication system, the crankshaft bearings are ball bearings and other components are designed with the low viscosity mixture in mind. Figure 5-7-7 shows the crankshaft bearings for a two stroke engine.

During the two-stroke inspection, check all lines and tanks that supply the gasoline/oil mix. For engines with an oil injection pump, make sure that your oil tank is sufficiently large so that if a full tank of fuel is burned, the engine will not run out of oil.

CAUTION: *This will severely damage the engine.*

Check that the control lever on the oil injection pump lines up with calibration marks to provide the right gasoline/oil mix.

Some two stroke engines have a separate engine oiler system for components that need a more viscous lubricant than what the 2-cycle mix can provide. On Rotax two-strokes, this system serves the rotary valve and water pump gears

Figure 5-7-6. Spectrographic analysis kit

Figure 5-7-7. Two-stroke engine crankshaft bearings.

Photo courtesy of SoLo Aviation

and was mentioned in Section 6 (Figure 5-6-2). An inspection of the oiler reservoir, usually a small plastic bottle mounted near the engine, should not reveal contamination or leaks, and should be filled to the proper level.

Section 8

Fuel System Inspection

The fuel system for LSA, like larger aircraft, includes the fuel tank(s), lines, valves, fuel pump(s), and fuel filters necessary to ensure a constant supply of fuel to the engine in most operating attitudes. A typical system is shown

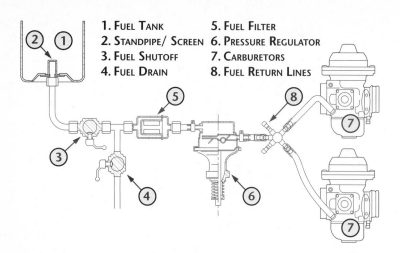

1. FUEL TANK
2. STANDPIPE/ SCREEN
3. FUEL SHUTOFF
4. FUEL DRAIN
5. FUEL FILTER
6. PRESSURE REGULATOR
7. CARBURETORS
8. FUEL RETURN LINES

Figure 5-8-1. Fuel Lines

Figure 5-8-2. Gascolator or fuel strainer bowl

in Figure 5-8-1. The system should be checked sequentially, starting with the tanks to verify that there are no restrictions to fuel flow. This can proceed as follows:

1. Check the fuel vents for proper operation.

2. The inside of the fuel tank should be visually inspected for signs of contamination or foreign object debris, especially around the fuel line outlet.

3. The gascolator, or fuel strainer bowl, should be removed, checked for contamination, cleaned and reinstalled with safety wiring as shown in Figure 5-8-2. If a fuel filter is installed, check for debris, replacement interval, and leaks.

4. Flexible fuel lines should be inspected from the tank to the engine for wear,

hardness, cracking, terminal fitting security, and incorrect attachment to the airframe. Fuel lines should never be directly mounted to the airframe because of vibration-induced wear; a method of supporting the line with a flexible stand-off (the ultralight community has been creative about this) needs to be employed. Clear fuel lines are more susceptible to hardening and UV damage, and require replacement on more frequent intervals than black, reinforced rubber lines.

5. Proper function of the fuel gauges (quantity and pressure) and the operation of the fuel system, vital to engine operation, should be verified.

If anomalies have been observed, the fuel system function can be checked by measuring fuel flow at the engine with the fuel pump "on" (if installed) and the fuel line disconnected. A target flow rate of 150% of full power fuel flow should be measured. This test would not be necessary unless there was a suspicion that something is restricting the flow, indicated by low fuel pressure at high power settings. Exercise extreme caution when working with gasoline; have a telephone and fire extinguisher within easy reach.

Section 9

Gearbox/Reduction Drive System

Many LSA are operating with a reduction drive to lower the engine r.p.m. so that a larger diameter, more efficient propeller can be used. In the case of geared reduction drives, such as shown in Figure 5-9-1, it is necessary to inspect the function of the gearbox since torque and vibration levels from the engine and propeller can be quite large. Engine manufacturers frequently install a torsional shock absorber, or damper, to help reduce the vibration levels. The damper is either a compliant bushing or a spring loaded device that connects the engine output shaft to the gearbox input and allows for a small amount of relative motion between the propeller and the engine. These dampers cannot usually be inspected without removing the gearbox, but their function can be tested by locking the engine and attempting to rotate the propeller by hand.

Manufacturers will specify the acceptable amount of rotation that the propeller will operate through with the engine locked (accomplished by installing the locking pin in the engine case) when a force is applied to the

Figure 5-9-1. Geared reduction system

propeller. The rotation should be smooth and without binding until the limit of travel, or torque, is reached.

In addition to testing the torsional damper, some engine installations include an overload clutch, or slipper clutch, that will reduce engine damage in the event of sudden propeller stoppage. These can be tested by again locking the engine and applying a torque to the propeller while noting torque values from a calibrated spring scale. Follow the manufacturer's recommendation on performing this functional test to ensure the full engine power can be delivered to the propeller.

Figure 5-9-2. Belt drive reduction system

Gear boxes should be serviced with gear oil if they are not an integral part of the engine block. The level should be checked, and if there is a magnetic plug, that should be removed and checked for the accumulation of metal particles. Refer to the manufacturer's specifications on quantity and type of gear oil (again, only if the gearbox is separate of the engine crankcase). When the propeller is rocked back and forth, there should be a small amount of freeplay and no binding in the motion. Any unusual noises as the propeller is moved would indicate bearing or gear failure.

A belt drive reduction system is shown in Figure 5-9-2. These systems are simpler to inspect than a gearbox since the entire system is usually exposed for view. The belt should be checked for the proper amount of tension, and no visible cracks or wear should be seen in the outside of the belt or at the roots of the belt teeth, if applicable. The prop bearings should be checked for proper operation by assessing any freeplay or noise that may occur as the prop is rotated.

Section 10

Propellers

Operation. The propeller converts engine power into aircraft power by accelerating a mass of air rearward which forces the airplane forward. Propeller theory is the combination of two other theories: *blade element theory* and *momentum theory*. Blade element theory states that a propeller can be analyzed as a series of elements from the root of the propeller to the tip, where each element sees a unique angle

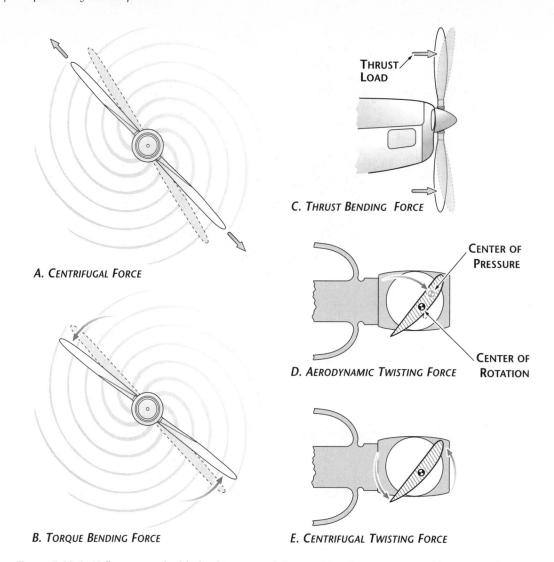

A. CENTRIFUGAL FORCE

B. TORQUE BENDING FORCE

THRUST LOAD

C. THRUST BENDING FORCE

CENTER OF PRESSURE

CENTER OF ROTATION

D. AERODYNAMIC TWISTING FORCE

E. CENTRIFUGAL TWISTING FORCE

Figure 5-10-1. Airflow around a blade element and the resulting forces generated by a propeller

of attack based on the rotational velocity, the incoming "induced" velocity of the air entering the propeller, and the twist angle of the propeller. Each blade element generates a certain amount of lift and drag, like a wing, which can be converted into an increment of power and thrust at a given radius on the propeller. Figure 5-10-1 shows a vector diagram of the airflow around a blade element and the resulting forces generated by a propeller. By adding all of the

Figure 5-10-2. Laminated wood propeller

contributions of the blade elements together, the total power and thrust can be determined.

The velocity of the incoming air into the propeller is a function of the thrust that is produced, which is the basis of momentum theory. Because the thrust cannot be determined until the incoming air velocity is known (blade element), and the incoming air is a function of the thrust produced (momentum theory), both theories are employed to find the operating point of the propeller. Once the operating point if found, the efficiency of the propeller can be determined by comparing the *power input* of the engine to the *power output* of the propeller, which is expressed as *Power = Thrust x Velocity*. Most propellers operate somewhere between 70% and 87% efficiency, depending on the speed of the aircraft and the rotational speed of the propeller.

Propellers are subject to several different forces including gyroscopic, centrifugal, and the aerodynamic loads that generate thrust. In addition to these forces, modes of vibration can occur due to the relatively thin cross section of the blades and the vibrational environment that a propeller operates in. As the blade flexes, additional stresses can be induced which may cause failure if the propeller is operated under these conditions for prolonged periods. Aircraft frequently have placards that limit continuous operation at certain engine speeds (r.p.m.) which may cause excessive vibration in the propeller. These speed ranges should be adhered to and may be felt in the cockpit as the vibration level increases when the engine r.p.m. is within the restricted range.

Types of Propellers

Propellers, like airframes, can have a variety of designs and construction styles that are optimized for a particular application. Below is a list of the most common styles and materials used in propellers:

Laminated wood. The laminated wood propeller shown in Figure 5-10-2 represents the oldest propeller design, essentially the same construction used by the Wright brothers in 1903. A wooden propeller has the advantage of high damping to minimize vibration, and it is not subject to fatigue failure as a metal propeller would be. Wood propellers will either have a metal sheath or an impact resistant plastic or epoxy composite layer to minimize damage from stones that might be sucked into the blades of the propeller. Wood propellers should be left in a horizontal position after flying to keep the prop in balance, as a small amount of moisture and resin in the wood will gravitate downward when the airplane is parked. Wood is commonly used for LSA propellers.

Composite. A composite propeller is shown in Figure 5-10-3. These propellers have recently become very popular since they are lighter than wooden propellers and have higher damping than aluminum propellers, reducing vibration. Construction can either be all composite, or there may be a wood core that has been covered with composites. Because composites are easy to shape, unique blade and tip designs are often found on these props to optimize performance.

Aluminum. The aluminum propeller is shown in Figure 5-10-4. Few of these are found on LSA, perhaps due to the investment cost to begin production and the recently discovered advantages of composite propellers. These propellers are heavier than wood or composite designs, but are stronger and do not require a tip treatment as a composite or wood propeller would require.

Ground adjustable pitch. The newer composite propellers are frequently designed with

Figure 5-10-3. Composite propeller

Figure 5-10-4. Aluminum propeller

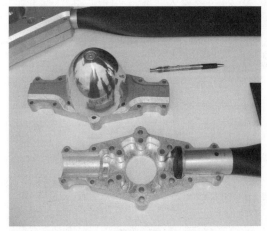

Figure 5-10-5. Root of one blade of a three bladed, ground adjustable propeller

ground adjustable pitch control. This has the advantage of allowing a single propeller design to be used in a variety of applications. Figure 5-10-5 shows the root of one blade in the hub of a ground adjustable propeller.

Figure 5-10-6. Decay

Figure 5-10-7. Delamination

Figure 5-10-8. Cracks in a blade initially appear as fine line in the paint.

Propeller Inspection – Wood Blades

As with all propellers, damage to the leading edge due to the ingestion of rocks and debris should be the first area of inspection. Erosion of the leading edge and larger dents and nicks should be examined and treated according to the manufacturer's recommendations. Wood propellers frequently have a metal cuff on the leading edge to reduce the likelihood of damage, and an inspection of this guard should ensure that it has not loosened or moved. The high centrifugal forces and high speeds at the outer region of the propeller create a severe environment, and inspections should include nicks, cracks, scratches, bruises, and other impact damage that could degrade the integrity of the cuff and its attachment.

Defects in wood include cracks, dents, warpage, glue failure, delamination and finish failure. Wood will degrade in the presence of moisture, and examples of decay and delamination are shown in Figures 5-10-6 and 5-10-7, respectively. Moisture not only causes decay and delamination, it will also cause the propeller to change dimension and weight which can affect the torque on the bolts and propeller balance. A changing moisture content due to seasonal changes requires that the bolt torque on wooden propellers be frequently checked, at least every 50 hours of operation.

Cracks can be detected by grasping the tip of the propeller and giving the blade a slight twist while examining for any relative motion that may indicate separation. Cracks usually start at the leading edge due to the severity of the environment, and may appear as a fine line in the paint as shown in Figure 5-10-8. Situations like this are critical and require immediate attention, usually replacement of the propeller.

Propeller Inspection – Composite Blades

Like wood blades, composite blades are frequently protected by a metal cuff on the leading edge which may be as simple as metal tape. Metal tape can develop wrinkles with time, as shown in Figure 5-10-9, and if this happens replacement is necessary due to the fact that the airflow becomes disturbed and will induce vibration in the propeller. The leading edge should be carefully inspected for nicks, dents, scratches and other signs of impact damage that may result in delamination, as shown in Figure 5-10-10. When a composite propeller delaminates, it is usually catastrophic and so surface damage needs to be taken seriously.

Similar to other composite structures, composite blades can be visually inspected by shining a light down the length of the blade and looking for bubbling or other defects in the surface finish. Typical damage found in this manner may be delamination or crazing. Some composite propellers have a pitch adjustment feature embedded in the blade which is actuated at the hub. In these cases, abnormal vibration may be an indication of a failure of the pitch adjustment device.

If the propeller has impacted a foreign object and caused a defect large enough to require repair but not large enough to reject the propeller, the manufacturer must be consulted before any repair work is performed. Again, due to the high centrifugal forces and necessity for balance, structural repairs must be approved by the manufacturer to ensure safe operation.

Figure 5-10-9. Metal tape with wrinkles

Propeller Inspection – Aluminum Blades

Aluminum blades are not common on LSA, but because of their popularity with general aviation, the effects of damage are well understood. Erosion on the tip is common due to the ingestion of small particles, usually occurring during taxi and takeoff. This type of damage creates small pits or nicks due to the high impact velocity of a foreign object with the passing blade, shown in Figure 5-10-11. In general, nicks that appear on the outer $1/3$ of the blade should be considered more serious because of the larger stresses that are experienced.

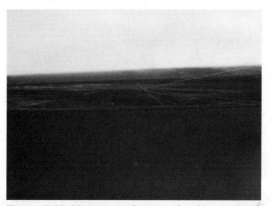

Figure 5-10-10. Impact damage that has resulted in delamination

Aluminum blades that suffer more severe damage in the form of leading edge pits can sometimes be repaired by blending the defect out with careful filing as specified by the manufacturer. Larger nicks, cuts or scratches may induce stress risers that result in fatigue cracking through the blade, and this usually results in a sudden failure with possibly catastrophic results for the airplane. These larger defects should be considered serious enough to warrant immediate grounding until the propeller is replaced or repaired.

Propeller Inspection – Other Inspection Items

Figure 5-10-11. Pits and nicks in aluminum prop blade

On ground adjustable propellers, the integrity of the blade/hub connection should be verified by attempting to move the blade in all directions (forward, backward, and twisting) while observing the motion at the hub. Any freeplay observed at the hub should be checked with the manufacturer's specification to determine if the propeller is airworthy.

Excessive propeller vibration can be caused by an imbalance between the blades or a single blade with an out-of-tolerance pitch. A very small error in pitch (fractions of a degree) can cause excessive vibration, and this should always be considered when troubleshooting vibration problems.

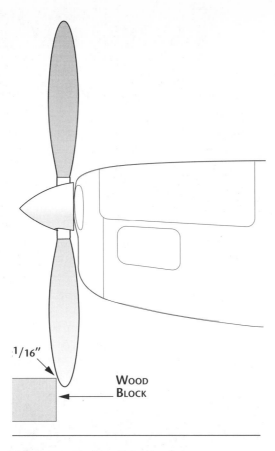

1/16"

WOOD
BLOCK

Figure 5-10-12. Measuring track

The propeller hub and propeller flange extending from the engine should be inspected for loose bolts, cracks and wear. Safety wiring on propeller bolts should be checked if required. Keeping in mind that the engine will move considerably during the start-up when the engine is firing at a low r.p.m., check the space between the prop hub and the cowl to ensure there is no interference. Propeller spinners and bulkheads are subject to cracking due to the high vibration environment that they operate in. Pay careful attention to all stress risers (screw and bolt holes) in the prop spinner and bulkheads, and carefully inspect for fatigue cracks radiating from these areas, similar to the example in Chapter 3, Figure 3-2-23.

An easy diagnostic check of the health of the drivetrain and propeller can be performed by measuring the blade track. Blade track refers to the accuracy of the blades rotating in a single plane, and any deviation from this plane can be the result of propeller or propeller shaft damage, resulting in vibration or failure of the propeller or drive system. To measure track, the aircraft should be chocked so it cannot be moved, and a block of wood is placed on the ground next to the propeller so that the propeller is almost touching the wood. As the propeller is slowly rotated (by hand, with the engine disabled so as to not fire), the relative

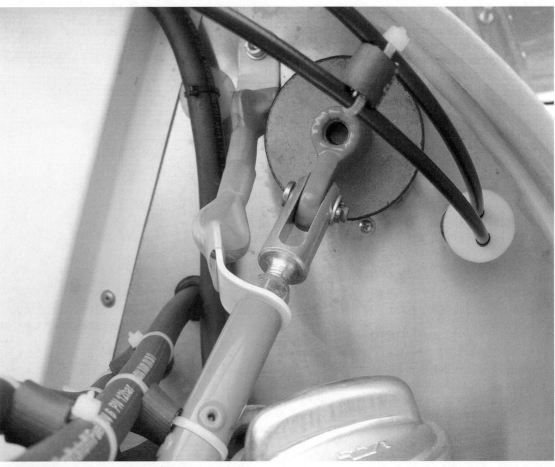

Figure 5-11-1. Engine mount safety strap

position of the propeller to the block is noted, and any deviations greater than ¹/₈″ may indicate a damaged system. Figure 5-10-12 shows the general procedure.

Section 11

Engine Mount and Controls

The engine mount carries high static and dynamic (vibration) loads from the engine to the airframe, and because of its critical nature, needs to be thoroughly inspected. Most engine mounts, regardless of the composition of the airplane and design of the engine, are made from welded steel tube. The inspection procedure presented in Chapter 3 for welded steel tube fuselages applies here. Some engine mounts on newer LSA have straps that positively attach the mount to the firewall in the event that a severe vibration in the engine might cause the entire mount to separate from the airframe. Figure 5-11-1 shows this.

In addition to the welded steel tube structure, the engine mount bushings that absorb engine vibrations should be inspected for cracking, sagging, stiffening, and tearing that may compromise their function. Engine mounts do not last forever, and if vibrations become a problem in the cockpit, the mounts are a good place to start looking. Engine mounts, such as the installation shown in Figure 5-11-2, can be evaluated by a visual and tactile inspection.

The controls that operate the engine are as important to safe flight as the function of the engine itself. On more than one occasion an airplane has experienced an unscheduled landing due to an improperly connected throttle cable which failed. Rotax has decided that the danger of a disconnected throttle cable warrants a spring to be placed on the throttle control to force it wide open (for the 9xx series motors) in the event that the control cable fails. This is not the case for Lycoming or Continental engines, where if the cable breaks, the throttle may move in any direction.

In an inspection of the engine controls, the springs, cables and mounting hardware should

Figure 5-11-2. Engine mounts

Figure 5-11-3. Inspect engine controls, springs, cables and mounting hardware for proper operation.

be checked for proper operation. Figure 5-11-3 shows the variety of parts to inspect to ensure proper engine control: bellcranks (L-brackets) for proper orientation, cable stops, springs, safety wiring, ferrules and plastic bushings, wire ties, guides and cable ties. Full travel of the throttle and mixture controls (where applicable) should be verified with an operator in the cockpit and an observer witnessing the control function at the engine.

Index